CONTENTS

S0-AFI-216

Contents
Chemistry, SV 0424-7

INTRODUCTION

This book is designed to serve a variety of needs and interests for teachers, students, parents, and tutors. The contents of this book are based upon both state and national standards. Teachers can use this book for review and remediation. Students will find the content to be concise and focused on the major concepts of the discipline. Parents can use this book to help their children with topics that may be posing a problem in the classroom. Tutors can use the material as a basis for their lessons and for assigning problems and questions.

Each unit follows the same sequence in covering a major topic. Each unit opens with Key Terms, which include all the boldfaced terms and their definitions presented in the same order as they are introduced in the text. As a result, the reader can develop a sense of the topics that are covered in the unit. The unit follows with a clear and concisely written text, which is divided into several sections. Each section is written so that the reader is not overwhelmed with details but rather guided through the topic in a logical sequence. Each unit then moves on to a Review, which consists of several multiple-choice and short-answer questions. The questions follow the same sequence as the material presented in the unit. As a result, the reader can easily locate the section where a review may be needed. Each unit concludes with a series of activities. These activities are designed to assess the reader's understanding of the content and to apply the information learned to novel situations. As a change of pace, some of the activities are meant to engage the reader in a "fun-type" exercise using a crossword puzzle or other similar device as a way of reinforcing the content. The book concludes with a Glossary, which lists all the boldfaced terms in alphabetical order, and an Answer Key, which gives the answers to all the activity questions.

This book has been designed and written so that teachers, students, parents, and tutors will all find it easy to use and follow. Most importantly, students will benefit from this book by achieving at a higher level in class and on standardized tests.

UNIT 1 — Structure and Properties of Matter

Chemistry is the study of **matter**. Everything in the universe, including Earth, this book, and even you, is made of matter. Scientists define matter as anything that has **mass** and **volume**. Volume is the space an object occupies. Mass is the amount of matter in an object or substance. Mass is different from **weight**. The weight of an object is defined as the force produced by gravity acting on an object. The mass of an object is constant. In other words, the mass of an object, such as an astronaut, is the same no matter whether he or she is on Earth or the moon. In contrast, the weight of an object varies, depending on its location. An astronaut weighs much less on the moon where the force of gravity is much less than it is on Earth.

States of Matter

Most of the matter you encounter is in one of three states. These three states of matter include *solids*, *liquids*, and *gases*. The state of matter depends on how the particles that make up the object or substance are arranged. The particles in a solid are held tightly in a rigid structure. They are not free to move about but can only vibrate slightly in their fixed positions. As a result, a solid has a fixed volume and a fixed shape.

The particles in a liquid are not held as tightly as those in a solid. As a result, the particles in a liquid

Key Terms

matter—anything that has mass and takes up space

mass—the amount of matter in an object or substance

volume—a measure of the size of a body or region in three-dimensional space

weight—a measure of the gravitational force exerted on an object

heat—the energy transferred between objects that are at different temperatures

temperature—a measure of how hot or cold something is

kinetic energy—the movement of particles

vapor pressure—the partial pressure exerted by a vapor that is in equilibrium with its liquid state at a given temperature

element—a substance that cannot be separated or broken down into simpler substances by ordinary means

compound—a substance made up of atoms of two or more different elements joined by chemical bonds

mixture—a combination of two or more substances that are not chemically combined

physical change—a change of matter from one form to another without a change in chemical properties

chemical change—a change that occurs when one or more substances change into entirely new substances with different properties

endothermic process—a process in which heat is absorbed from the environment

exothermic process—a process in which a substance releases heat into the environment

can move freely and slide past one another. Therefore, a liquid has a fixed volume but not a fixed shape. A liquid always takes the shape of the container that holds it. For example, the same volume of milk will have a different shape, depending on whether it is in a large glass or a small pot.

The particles in a gas move at high speeds and independently of one another. This freedom to move about results from the very weak forces of attraction that exist between gas particles. As a result of these weak attractive forces, a gas has neither a fixed volume nor a fixed shape. A gas always takes the volume and shape of the container which holds it. For example, the same amount of a gas will have both a different shape and a different volume, depending on whether the gas is in a small, round balloon or in a large, square room.

Heat and Temperature

The state of matter of an object can change. A familiar example involves water. A piece of solid ice left on a countertop will slowly melt and change into a liquid. Eventually, the liquid will gradually disappear as the particles evaporate to form a gas. Matter undergoes a change in state because **heat** is either released or absorbed. Heat is defined as the energy that is transferred between objects that are at different temperatures. Heat is always transferred from a warmer object to a cooler object. For example, an ice cube in your hand melts because heat is transferred from your hand, which is warmer, to the ice cube, which is cooler. However, an ice cube does not melt in a freezer because heat is not transferred between two objects that have the same temperature.

Although the terms heat and **temperature** are often used together, they are not the same. Heat is the energy that is transferred between objects at

different temperatures. The warmer object releases energy as heat. The cooler object absorbs heat as energy. The particles in the warmer object move more slowly as they release energy as heat. The particles in the cooler object move more rapidly as they absorb energy as heat. The movement of particles is known as **kinetic energy**. While heat is energy that is transferred, temperature is actually a measurement. Temperature is the measurement of the average kinetic energy of the random motion of particles in an object or substance. Temperature is expressed using different scales. These scales include the Fahrenheit scale, which is not used in chemistry, and two other scales that are used in chemistry—the Celsius scale and the Kelvin scale. Changing between the Celsius and Kelvin scales involves either adding or subtracting 273. For example:

$$27°C = 300 \text{ K} \qquad 27 + 273 = 300$$
$$290 \text{ K} = 17°C \qquad 290 - 273 = 17$$

The transfer of heat between two objects does not always affect the temperature. For example, if you place a thermometer in a pot of water that is being heated, you will notice that the temperature slowly rises. The temperature rises because the average kinetic energy (random motion) of the water particles increases as they absorb energy as heat. However, as you continue to heat the water, you will notice that the temperature does not increase as the water boils and turns into a gas, which we commonly call steam. At this point, the energy being added as heat is being used to move the particles away from each other. In other words, the energy being added as heat is used to move the particles of water farther apart so that they form a gas.

Liquids and Vapor Pressure

If you open a bottle of rubbing alcohol, you can smell the alcohol. Some of the alcohol particles have enough kinetic energy to escape the liquid and turn into a gas. These gas particles are the alcohol you smell. When you replace the cap on the bottle, the liquid particles can no longer escape. Instead, the gas particles remain inside the bottle, pushing against the inside of the container. As they push against the inside, the gas particles exert a pressure on the walls of the container. The pressure they exert is called the **vapor pressure**. Vapor is another term for gas.

If the temperature of a liquid increases, the particles will have more kinetic energy. As a result, more of the liquid particles can escape and form a vapor. The more vapor present, the higher the vapor pressure. Therefore, the vapor pressure of a liquid increases as the temperature of a liquid increases.

The gases that make up the air also exert a pressure. This is known as atmospheric pressure. Standard atmospheric pressure is 760 mm of mercury, which is also equal to 1 atmosphere of pressure. When the vapor pressure of a liquid equals atmospheric pressure, the liquid turns into a vapor. Therefore, the boiling point of a liquid can be defined as the temperature at which the vapor pressure equals the atmospheric pressure.

Gas Laws

Gas particles may move about in a random fashion. However, gas particles obey certain laws. One is Boyle's law. This law states that the volume of a fixed amount of gas at a constant temperature increases as the pressure on the gas decreases. Conversely, Boyle's law also states that the volume of a fixed amount of gas at a constant temperature decreases as the pressure on the gas increases. The relationship between volume and pressure as stated in Boyle's law is an inverse one. As the pressure decreases, the volume increases. As the pressure increases, the volume decreases.

Boyle's law can be stated as an equation:

$$P_1V_1 = P_2V_2$$

where P_1 and V_1 are the pressure and volume under one set of conditions, and P_2 and V_2 are the pressure and volume under another set of conditions.

Another gas law is Charles's law. This law states that the volume of a fixed amount of a gas at constant pressure increases as the temperature of the gas increases. Conversely, Charles's law also states that the volume of a fixed amount of a gas at constant pressure decreases as the temperature of the gas decreases. The relationship between volume and temperature as stated in Charles's law is a direct one.

As the temperature increases, the volume increases. As the temperature decreases, the volume decreases. Charles's law can be stated as an equation:

$$\frac{V_1}{T_1} = \frac{V_2}{T_2}$$

where V_1 and T_1 are the volume and temperature under one set of conditions, and V_2 and T_2 are the volume and temperature under another set of conditions.

Boyle's law and Charles's law are sometimes combined to show what happens when both the temperature and pressure of a gas are changed. This is known as the combined gas law. The following equation shows the combined gas law.

$$\frac{P_1V_1}{T_1} = \frac{P_2V_2}{T_2}$$

Note that the above equation includes six quantities. Five of them must be given, and then the equation must be rearranged to solve for the unknown quantity.

Elements, Compounds, and Mixtures

Matter exists in many different forms. Scientists recognize that classifying matter in groups makes it easier to study and understand. You have learned one way to classify matter—either as a solid, liquid, or gas. Another way to classify matter is as an element, compound, or mixture. An **element** is defined as any substance that cannot be broken down into a simpler substance by ordinary means. Only 113 elements are known. Gold is one. Gold is classified as an element because it cannot be changed into a simpler substance by ordinary means, such as heating it or hammering it. Heating can change gold from a solid to a liquid, but it is still gold. Hammering it can change gold into a very thin layer known as gold leaf but it is still gold. Gold can be found on Earth as an element. Prospectors use screens to filter tiny gold particles from streams and rivers.

A **compound** is a substance made up of two or more different elements that are chemically joined. In addition to being found as an element, gold can also be found chemically joined with other elements in ores. Mining companies use heat or electricity to separate the other elements from the gold. Once separated, the gold is an element and is commonly called pure gold.

A **mixture** is a combination of two or more substances that are not chemically joined to one another. In its pure form as an element, gold is too soft to make jewelry. Pure gold is known as 24-karat gold. A lot of jewelry is made from 18-karat gold, which is made by mixing 18 grams of gold with 6 grams of other elements, such as silver, copper, or nickel. The gold used to make jewelry is an *alloy*, which is a mixture made of a metal, such as gold, mixed with one or more other elements.

An alloy is an example of a *homogeneous mixture*. In a homogenous mixture, the substances are distributed uniformly or evenly throughout the mixture. Sugar dissolved in water is another example of a homogenous mixture. Sand that settles to the bottom of a jar of water is an example of a *heterogeneous mixture*. In a heterogeneous mixture, the substances are not uniformly distributed.

Different methods are required to separate the components of a compound from those of a mixture. Because the substances in a compound are chemically joined, then a chemical process must be used to separate them. However, because the components in a mixture are not chemically joined, then a physical process is all that is needed to separate them. For example, a mixture of sand and water can be separated by filtering it. A mixture of two liquids can be separated if they have different boiling points. Keep in mind that heat can also be used to separate the components of a compound. Heating the compound can break apart the chemical bonds that hold together the various components in the compound.

Physical and Chemical Changes

Chemistry is the study of matter and how it changes. A change in matter can be either physical or chemical. A **physical change** does not involve any change in the identity of a substance. For example, melting wax, dissolving sugar in coffee, and filtering water to drink are examples of a physical change. In none of these examples does the identity of the substance change. Melted wax is still wax. Cooling it can return it to its original condition.

A **chemical change** occurs when one or more substances change into entirely new substances with different properties. A chemical change occurs whenever a new substance is made. In other words, a *chemical reaction* has taken place. Burning a candle is an example of a chemical change. Once the candle has burned to produce new substances, there is no way to change these new substances back into wax.

Both physical and chemical changes involve changes in energy. For example, it takes energy as heat to melt wax. In this case, the particles of wax absorb energy as they change from a solid into a liquid. Any change in matter in which energy is absorbed is known as an **endothermic process**. Endothermic describes a process in which heat is absorbed from the environment. The boiling of water is another example of a physical change that is an endothermic process.

A burning candle is an example of an **exothermic process**. Exothermic describes a process in which one or more substances release heat into the environment. The freezing of water is an example of a physical change that is an exothermic process.

All physical and chemical changes are accompanied by a change in energy. A physical change may be either endothermic or exothermic. Water turning into a vapor is an example of a physical change which is endothermic. Water vapor turning into a liquid is an example of a physical change which is exothermic. Similarly, a chemical change can be either endothermic or exothermic. When barium hydroxide and ammonium nitrate, two chemical substances, are mixed in a glass beaker, ice crystals will form on the beaker. This is an example of a chemical change which is endothermic. When a piece of sodium metal is dropped into water, an explosion occurs that releases heat and light. This is an example of a chemical change which is exothermic.

UNIT 1

Review

Darken the circle by the best answer.

1. Matter that has a fixed volume but does not have a fixed shape is
   - Ⓐ a solid.
   - Ⓑ a liquid.
   - Ⓒ a gas.
   - Ⓓ either a liquid or a gas.

2. Which statement is true concerning temperature?
   - Ⓐ Temperature and heat are the same.
   - Ⓑ Temperature can be measured in only one scale.
   - Ⓒ Temperature is a measurement of the average kinetic energy of the particles in a substance.
   - Ⓓ Both the Fahrenheit and Celsius scales are used by scientists when recording temperatures.

3. Which temperature equals 0°C?
   - Ⓐ 273 K
   - Ⓑ 273°F
   - Ⓒ −273 K
   - Ⓓ 0 K

4. With respect to gases, Boyle's law shows the relationship between
   - Ⓐ volume and temperature.
   - Ⓑ temperature and pressure.
   - Ⓒ pressure and volume.
   - Ⓓ volume, temperature, and pressure.

5. According to Charles's law, the volume of a gas will increase when the
   - Ⓐ amount of gas in a sealed container is increased.
   - Ⓑ pressure is decreased.
   - Ⓒ temperature is decreased.
   - Ⓓ temperature is increased.

6. Which is best classified as a heterogeneous mixture?
   - Ⓐ slice of pizza
   - Ⓑ gold bracelet
   - Ⓒ hot tea
   - Ⓓ pure water

7. A new substance is produced as a result of a(n)
   - Ⓐ physical change.
   - Ⓑ chemical change.
   - Ⓒ endothermic process.
   - Ⓓ exothermic process.

8. Explain how an endothermic process differs from an exothermic process.

   _____

   _____

   _____

9. Explain the difference between a physical change and a chemical change.

   _____

   _____

   _____

UNIT 1

States of Matter

Scientists often use models in their search for answers and solutions. For example, models can be used to represent the various states of matter. Examine the following models which show the arrangements of particles in different samples of matter.

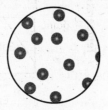

model A

model B

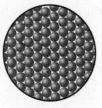

model C

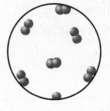

model D

1. Which model(s) can represent a liquid? Explain the reason for your choice(s).

_____

_____

2. In which model(s) do the particles remain in fixed positions? Explain the reason for your choice(s).

_____

_____

3. Which model(s) can represent a sample of matter that has neither a fixed shape nor a fixed volume?

_____

_____

4. What will happen to the volume and shape of the matter represented by model B when it is placed in a container with a different volume and shape?

_____

_____

UNIT 1

Heat and Temperature

Heat is the energy that is transferred between objects that are at different temperatures.

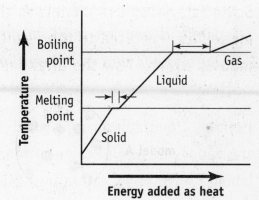

Examine the graph which shows what happens to a sample of matter as energy is added as heat.

Use the graph to answer the questions.

1. Explain how this graph supports the statement that the transfer of energy as heat does not always affect the temperature.

   _____

   _____

2. Why does the temperature increase as the liquid is heated?

   _____

   _____

3. Why doesn't the temperature increase as the liquid changes into a gas?

   _____

   _____

4. What states of matter are present at the melting point?

   _____

5. Where would the freezing point be located on this graph?

   _____

6. What would happen to the temperature while the gas is cooled and condenses into a liquid?

   _____

   _____

UNIT 1

Liquids and Vapor Pressure

> *Vapor is another term for gas. Vapor pressure is the partial pressure exerted by a vapor that is in equilibrium with its liquid state at a given temperature.*

Examine the graph at right which shows the vapor pressure of three different liquids, labeled A, B, and C, at various temperatures. Notice that the unit used for vapor pressure is mm Hg, or millimeters of mercury. The chemical symbol for mercury is Hg.

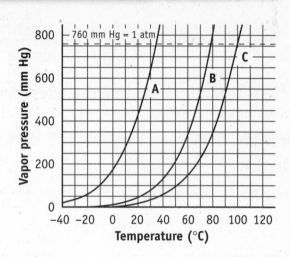

Use the graph to answer the questions.

1. What do all three liquids have in common? _____

2. Which liquid is first to form a vapor as the temperature increases? _____

3. What is the vapor pressure of liquid A at 20°C? _____

4. At what temperature does liquid B have a vapor pressure of 250 mm Hg? _____

5. What is the boiling point of liquid B? _____

6. Water normally boils at 100°C. Which liquid on this graph represents water? _____

7. Which liquid(s) still form vapor even at 0°C, the freezing point of water? _____

8. What must be the temperature change so that the vapor pressure of liquid C decreases from 550 mm Hg to 450 mm Hg? _____

9. Which liquid shows the greatest change in vapor pressure when the temperature is raised from 0°C to 20°C? _____

10. Draw a curve on the graph for the following data. Label your graph liquid D.

Temperature (°C)	−20	0	20	40	80	95
Vapor pressure (mm Hg)	125	150	198	249	410	520

Unit 1, Structure and Properties of Matter
Chemistry, SV 0424-7

UNIT 1

Boyle's Law

> **Boyle's Law states that for a fixed amount of gas at a constant temperature**
> • *the volume of the gas increases as the pressure of the gas decreases, and*
> • *the volume of the gas decreases as the pressure of the gas increases.*
>
> **Formula: $P_1V_1 = P_2V_2$**

Examine the graph at right which illustrates what happens to a volume of gas as the pressure changes at constant temperature. The unit used for volume is liter (L), and the unit used for pressure is kilopascal (kPa).

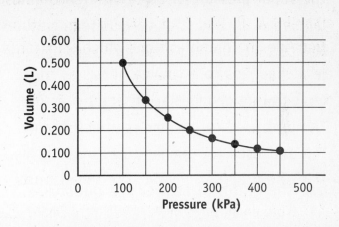

Use the graph to answer the questions.

1. Explain how this graph supports Boyle's law.

_____

_____

_____

_____

2. What happens to the volume of the gas as the pressure is doubled from 100 kPa to 200 kPa?

_____

_____

3. Which change in pressure causes the largest change in volume?

_____

_____

4. Use the shape of the graph to *estimate* what the volume of the gas would be if the pressure were increased to 550 kPa.

_____

_____

5. Use the data from the graph to *calculate* what the volume of the gas would be if the pressure were increased to 550 kPa.

6. Take any two points on the graph and show how they demonstrate Boyle's law as represented by the formula $P_1V_1 = P_2V_2$.

UNIT 1

Charles's Law

Charles's Law states that for a fixed amount of gas at a constant pressure,
- **the volume of the gas increases as the temperature of the gas increases, and**
- **the volume of the gas decreases as the temperature of the gas decreases.**

Formula: $\dfrac{V_1}{T_1} = \dfrac{V_2}{T_2}$

Examine the graph at right which illustrates what happens to a volume of gas as the temperature changes at constant pressure. The unit used for volume is liter (L), and the unit used for temperature is kelvin (K).

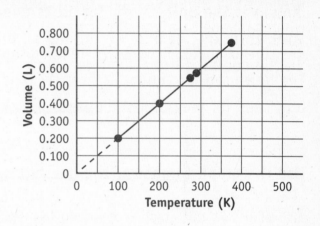

Use the graph to answer the questions.

1. Explain how this graph supports Charles's law.

_____

2. What happens to the volume of the gas as the temperature is doubled from 100 K to 200 K?

_____

3. Use the dotted line on the graph to *predict* what the volume of the gas would be if the temperature were 0 K, a value known as absolute zero.

_____

4. Use the data from the graph to *calculate* what the volume of the gas would be if the temperature were increased to 500 K.

5. Take any two points on the graph and show how they demonstrate Charles's law as represented by the formula $\dfrac{V_1}{T_1} = \dfrac{V_2}{T_2}$.

UNIT 1

Combined Gas Law

> The combined gas law shows what happens when both the temperature and pressure of a gas are changed.
>
> Formula: $\dfrac{P_1 V_1}{T_1} = \dfrac{P_2 V_2}{T_2}$

Use the combined gas law to complete the following table. Keep in mind that Kelvin is the unit to use for all temperature values. The unit for pressure can be atm, torr, kPa, or mm Hg as long as the same unit is used for both pressure values in the combined gas law equation.

P_1	V_1	T_1	P_2	V_2	T_2
600 mm Hg	24 mL	18°C	430 mm Hg		24°C
	1.6 L	25°C	1.2 atm	2.2 L	10°C
95 kPa	224 mL	374 K	125 kPa	450 mL	
760 torr	2.4 L	37°C		4.8 L	300 K
1.5 atm		−20°C	2.6 atm	750 mL	−5°C

UNIT 1 Elements, Compounds, and Mixtures

Find the answers in the word search puzzle.

```
O  L  J  Y  E  I  K  M  H  L  M  Q  U  T  W
U  F  A  S  U  O  E  N  E  G  O  M  O  H  A
M  Q  H  G  N  O  T  N  E  M  E  L  E  V  K
N  W  W  O  Y  U  H  G  S  P  T  T  Y  X  K
N  J  J  F  P  I  O  N  I  N  E  C  M  W  X
U  Y  V  J  X  U  Q  E  T  R  L  Y  C  P  X
M  I  L  J  R  H  Y  C  O  M  P  O  U  N  D
O  U  S  V  Q  C  I  G  I  J  U  V  F  B  M
W  U  R  M  I  O  E  X  J  G  R  N  A  U  P
I  A  H  Q  A  N  T  J  E  F  E  B  Y  Y  G
Z  Q  Q  T  E  U  X  J  F  S  G  M  H  B  B
H  Z  A  O  R  Q  H  G  F  V  O  Z  K  B  W
M  W  U  E  J  D  F  I  T  A  L  L  O  Y  R
E  S  I  N  N  M  E  J  W  N  D  J  K  A  K
A  H  B  B  P  X  G  J  L  T  H  N  R  B  I
```

1. cannot be broken down into a simpler substance by ordinary means
2. evenly dispersed
3. 24-karat gold
4. combination of two or more substances that are not chemically joined
5. combination of two or more substances that are chemically joined
6. a substance made by mixing two metals
7. unevenly dispersed

Unit 1, Structure and Properties of Matter
Chemistry, SV 0424-7

UNIT 1

Separation of Mixtures

> *A mixture is a combination of two or more substances that are not chemically joined to one another.*

Explain how you would separate the components in each of the following mixtures. A mixture is a combination of two or more substances that are not chemically joined and therefore can be separated by physical means.

1. the cashews in a bowl of mixed nuts _____

2. salt water _____

3. the pulp in orange juice _____

4. oil and water _____

5. pebbles buried in the sand _____

6. iron filings mixed with sand _____

7. salt and sand _____

8. the various metals in a 14-karat gold bracelet _____

9. marbles of various sizes _____

10. Iron filings are mixed with sulfur powder. A magnet can be used to remove the filings. However, after the mixture has been heated and then cooled, the iron is no longer attracted to a magnet and therefore cannot be separated. What do you conclude has happened?

_____

_____

_____

UNIT 1 Physical and Chemical Changes

> A physical change does not involve any change in the identity of a substance, such as melting wax.
>
> A chemical change occurs when one or more substances change into entirely new substances with different properties, such as burning a candle.

Identify each of the following as either a physical change or a chemical change.

1. A glass window shatters after being struck by a ball. _____

2. A rock is crushed to extract the gold.

   _____

3. Iron rusts. _____

4. Water droplets form on a cold glass. _____

5. Bleach is used to remove a stain from a shirt. _____

6. Oxygen and hydrogen gases are combined to make water. _____

7. A car engine burns gasoline. _____

8. Salt water evaporates so that only the salts remain. _____

9. The air is heated so that a hot-air balloon can take off. _____

10. Lightning changes some of the oxygen in air into ozone gas. _____

Identify each of the following changes as either an endothermic or exothermic process.

11. The sand on a beach gets hot from the sun.

    _____

12. Chemical reactions on the sun give off light and heat. _____

13. Water droplets form on the outside of a cold glass. _____

14. Water droplets evaporate from a countertop.

    _____

15. A match burns. _____

16. A piece of paper catches fire. _____

17. A car's engine burns gasoline. _____

18. A firework explodes in the air. _____

19. The air gets warmer from the exploding fireworks. _____

20. Ice cubes form in a freezer. _____

UNIT 2

Atoms and the Periodic Table

Nearly 2500 years ago, the ancient Greeks proposed that all matter is made of extremely small particles called atoms. Until recently, no one had ever seen an atom. The ancient Greeks based their ideas about atoms on reasoning and logic. Not until the 1700s did scientists begin to collect data that led to the development of the *atomic theory*. The atomic theory states that all matter is made of atoms. An **atom** is defined as the smallest unit of an element that retains all the properties of that element.

Parts of an Atom

In 1808, John Dalton, an English schoolteacher, studied the various experimental data that had been collected about atoms. He then looked at what the ancient Greeks had said about atoms. Piecing together all the information, Dalton developed the first modern atomic theory. Dalton's theory had one major advantage over all the earlier ideas about atoms. Dalton's theory could be tested by experiments. Some of what Dalton proposed was found to be correct.

Key Terms

atom—the smallest unit of an element that retains all the properties of that element

proton—a subatomic particle that has a positive charge, usually written as $+1$

neutron—a subatomic particle that is neutral

nucleus—the central region of an atom where the protons and neutrons are located

electron—a subatomic particle that has a negative charge, usually written as -1

atomic number—the number of protons an atom has

mass number—the total number of protons and neutrons of the nucleus

isotopes—atoms of the same element that have different numbers of neutrons

atomic mass—the unit used to express the mass of an atom or the mass of a subatomic particle

average atomic mass—a weighted average of the atomic masses of all the isotopes of an element

electron configuration—the description of how an atom's electrons orbit its nucleus

excited state—a state in which an electron has more energy than it does at its ground state

ground state—the state in which an electron has the lowest energy level available

period—a horizontal row in the periodic table

group—a vertical column in the periodic table

valence electron—an electron found in the outermost shell of an atom that determines the atom's chemical properties

ionization energy—the energy required to remove an electron from an atom

ion—an atom that has either lost or gained an electron

electronegativity—a measure of the ability of an atom in a chemical compound to attract electrons

Other parts of Dalton's theory were eventually replaced as new information about atoms was collected.

One of Dalton's proposals that was eventually discarded was his idea that an atom could not be divided into smaller particles. Today, scientists know that an atom can be divided into numerous smaller particles. Three major subatomic particles are now known. These three subatomic particles are the proton, the neutron, and the electron.

A **proton** is a subatomic particle that has a positive charge, usually written as $+1$. A **neutron** is a subatomic particle that is neutral. This neutral charge is usually written as 0. The protons and neutrons are located in the central region of an atom. This region is called the **nucleus**. A nucleus of an atom is the dense, central portion of an atom where all its protons and neutrons are located.

An **electron** is a subatomic particle that has a negative charge, usually written as -1. All atoms are electrically neutral because every atom has an equal number of protons and electrons. Unlike the protons and neutrons, electrons are located outside the nucleus. The current model of an atom shows electrons orbiting the nucleus, where the protons and neutrons are located.

The number of protons an atom has is known as its **atomic number**. For example, an oxygen atom has 8 protons. Therefore, the atomic number of oxygen is 8. Scientists use a shorthand notation for atoms. In this example, the shorthand notation for an oxygen atom is written as $_8O$. The letter O is the symbol for oxygen. The subscript represents the atomic number. Notice that this symbol tells you that an oxygen atom has 8 protons. Because all atoms are neutral, an oxygen atom also has 8 electrons.

Both a proton and a neutron have mass, although the quantity of mass each has is extremely small. The total number of protons and neutrons of the nucleus is known as an atom's **mass number**. Electrons are not included in an atom's mass number because the mass of an electron is so small that it can be disregarded. The mass number of an atom is written as a superscript. For example, the symbol for an oxygen atom is written as $_8^{16}O$. Notice that you can calculate that this oxygen atom has 8 neutrons by taking its mass number (protons and neutrons) and subtracting its atomic number (protons), or $16 - 8 = 8$.

Isotopes and Atomic Masses

The symbol for an oxygen atom can be written as either $_8^{16}O$ or $_8^{17}O$. Notice that both atoms have the same atomic number—8. Therefore, both atoms have 8 protons and 8 electrons. However, these two atoms have different atomic masses—16 and 17. Based on these atomic masses, an atom of $_8^{16}O$ has 8 neutrons while an atom of $_8^{17}O$ has 9 neutrons. Atoms of the same element that have different numbers of neutrons are called **isotopes**. Notice that all isotopes of an element have the same atomic number but different mass numbers.

Recall that mass numbers are based on the number of protons and neutrons in the nucleus of an atom. Masses are often expressed in the unit gram (g). However, atoms are so small that this unit would not be very convenient to use. For example, a copper atom has a mass of 0.00000000000000000000000010552 g. As a result, scientists use a different unit to express **atomic mass** for either the mass of an atom or the mass of a subatomic particle. This unit is the atomic mass unit (amu). A proton and neutron each have a mass of 1 amu.

Most elements are mixtures of isotopes. For example, carbon is found in nature as two stable isotopes, known as carbon-12 and carbon-13. The numbers 12 and 13 that follow the element's name represent each atom's atomic mass. The atomic number of carbon is 6. Therefore, carbon-12 has 6 protons, 6 electrons, and 6 neutrons. Carbon-13 has 6 protons, 6 electrons, and 7 neutrons.

Carbon-12 and carbon-13 are not present in nature in equal amounts. In fact, there is much more carbon-12 than there is carbon-13. Scientists take into account the relative abundance of each isotope when they refer to an atom's atomic mass. For example, the atomic mass of a carbon atom is recorded as 12.0107 amu. This value is the **average atomic mass**, which is a weighted average of the atomic masses of all the isotopes of an element.

To understand how to calculate a weighted average, consider how the average atomic mass of two isotopes of copper is calculated. One isotope is copper-63, which represents 69% of all the copper isotopes. The other isotope is copper-65, which represents the remaining 31% of all the copper isotopes. The average atomic mass of a copper atom is calculated as follows:

(63 amu × 0.69) + (65 amu × 0.31) = 63.62 amu

Electron Configurations

At first, models of an atom showed electrons orbiting the nucleus in much the same way as the planets orbit the sun. However, as scientists learned more about the structure of atoms, this model of the atom changed. Electrons are still pictured as orbiting the nucleus, but in a much more complex manner. The orbit an electron follows as it circles the nucleus is described in terms of energy levels, shells, and orbitals. An electron's orbit can also be described in terms of letters and numbers. This description is known as an **electron configuration**, which describes how an atom's electrons orbit its nucleus.

For example, consider hydrogen, which has the simplest atomic structure with only one electron. The electron configuration for hydrogen is written as $1s^1$. The superscript 1 indicates that hydrogen's one electron orbits the nucleus in an orbital that has a spherical (s) shape and is in the first (1) energy level. The first energy level can hold only two electrons. Therefore, any additional electrons must orbit in levels with higher energy. Consider lithium, which has three electrons. The electron configuration for lithium is written as $1s^2 2s^1$. Notice that lithium's third electron orbits the nucleus in an s orbital in the second energy level, represented by the coefficient 2.

An electron configuration can be written for an atom of any element, no matter how many electrons it has. An example is silver that has 47 electrons. Its electron configuration is written as:

$$1s^2 2s^2 2p^6 3s^2 3p^6 3d^{10} 4s^2 4p^6 4d^{10} 5s^1$$

Notice that these 47 electrons occupy five energy levels, which are represented by the coefficients 1, 2, 3, 4, and 5, and in three types of orbitals, which are represented by the letters s, p, and d.

Writing an electron configuration for an atom can be difficult, especially for one that has many electrons like silver. There are certain rules to follow.

1. An electron must occupy the lowest energy level available.
2. Each orbital can hold only a certain number of electrons. The s orbital can hold a maximum of 2 electrons, while the p orbital can hold 6 electrons, and the d orbital can hold as many as 10 electrons. Another orbital, known as the f orbital, can hold a maximum of 14 electrons.
3. Electrons fill orbitals that have the lowest energy first.

In some cases, an orbital that is in an energy level with a higher number may actually have less energy than an orbital in an energy level with a lower number. For example, an electron will occupy the 4s orbital before it occupies the 3d orbital because the 4s orbital actually has a lower energy level than the 3d orbital.

If an electron has enough energy, it can occupy an orbital with a higher energy level than it normally would. For example, again consider the element hydrogen. Recall that its electron configuration is written as $1s^1$. However, hydrogen's one electron can move, or jump, to an orbital that is at a higher energy level. In this case, the electron configuration may be written as $2s^1$. Notice that hydrogen's electron has jumped from the 1s orbital to the 2s orbital.

An electron that occupies a higher energy level although a lower energy level is available is said to be in the **excited state**. When all the electrons occupy the lowest energy levels available, they are said to be in the **ground state**. Therefore, $1s^1$ represents the ground state electron configuration for a hydrogen atom, while $2s^1$ represents an excited state. Can you see why the following electron configuration represents an excited state for a silver atom?

$$1s^2 2s^2 2p^6 3s^2 3p^6 3d^{10} 4s^2 4p^6 4d^9 5s^2$$

There is a simpler way to determine an electron configuration rather than trying to write it based on the rules. All you have to do is check a periodic table, which usually contains the electron configurations for all the elements.

Unit 2, Atoms and the Periodic Table
Chemistry, SV 0424-7

The Periodic Table

In 1869, a Russian chemist named Dmitri Mendeleev arranged the elements known at that time into a table. He wrote the symbol for each element on a card, along with its physical and chemical properties such as its average atomic mass. Looking at his table, Mendeleev recognized that the chemical properties of the elements repeated at regular intervals. Mendeleev had invented the first periodic table.

Today, a periodic table lists all the known 113 elements. The elements are arranged according to increasing atomic number. A periodic table starts with hydrogen, with atomic number 1, and ends with a newly-created element, whose symbol is Uuq, with atomic number 114. This symbol will eventually be changed when a group of chemists agree upon a name and new symbol for this element. By the way, an element with atomic number 113 has yet to be discovered or created.

A periodic table is arranged in rows and columns. A horizontal row is called a **period**. Elements in the same period have the same number of occupied energy levels. For example, all the elements in Period 3 have electrons that occupy three energy levels, extending to the $3s$, $3p$, and $3d$ orbitals. A vertical column on a periodic table is known as a **group**. The elements in a particular group have the same number of electrons in the outer energy level. These electrons are called **valence electrons**. For example, all elements in Group 1 have one valence electron, although not in the same energy level. Lithium (Li) and potassium (K) are members of Group 1. While lithium has its one valence electron in the second energy level, potassium has its one valence electron in the fourth energy level.

Some groups have names. Group 1 elements are called the alkali metals, Group 2 the alkaline-earth metals, Group 17 the halogens, and Group 18 the noble gases. The noble gases are a unique group because they are unreactive. Unlike the other elements, the noble gases tend not to react because they have a full set of valence electrons.

Most elements are metals. These elements share many properties, especially their ability to conduct electricity. The right side of a periodic table contains the nonmetals, most of which are gases. Between the metals and nonmetals lie the metalloids, also known as semiconductors. These elements conduct electricity better than nonmetals but not as well as metals. The best known metalloid is silicon (Si), which is used to make computer chips.

In proceeding across a period or down a group, you would also notice certain trends. For example, the **ionization energy** decreases as you move down a group. In contrast, the ionization energy increases as you move across a period. Ionization energy is the energy required to remove an electron from an atom. An atom that has either lost or gained an electron is called an **ion**.

Atomic size also follows a periodic trend. The atomic radius increases as you move down a group. In contrast, the atomic radius decreases as you move across a period. Still another trend can be seen with respect to **electronegativity**, which is a measure of the ability of an atom in a chemical compound to attract electrons.

UNIT 2

Review

Darken the circle by the best answer.

1. The number of protons in an atom equals the
   - (A) number of neutrons.
   - (B) mass number.
   - (C) number of isotopes.
   - (D) number of electrons.

2. How many neutrons are present in an atom that has an atomic number of 62 and a mass number of 151?
   - (A) 62
   - (B) 89
   - (C) 151
   - (D) 213

3. Isotopes differ in their
   - (A) atomic numbers.
   - (B) number of protons.
   - (C) atomic mass numbers.
   - (D) both atomic numbers and atomic mass numbers.

4. An atom of potassium-39
   - (A) cannot have any other isotopes.
   - (B) contains 39 electrons.
   - (C) contains a total of 39 neutrons and protons.
   - (D) has an atomic number of 39.

5. The average atomic mass of an element is closest to the isotope of that element that
   - (A) is most abundant.
   - (B) is least abundant.
   - (C) has the greatest atomic mass.
   - (D) has the most protons.

6. Which electron configuration shows an electron in an excited state?
   - (A) $1s^2 2s^2 2p^6 3s^2 3p^6 3d^{10} 4s^2 4p^6$
   - (B) $1s^2 2s^2 2p^6 3s^2 3p^5 3d^{10} 4s^2 4p^6$
   - (C) $1s^2 2s^2 2p^6 3s^2 3p^6$
   - (D) $1s^2 2s^2 2p^6 3s^2 3p^6 3d^{10} 4s^1$

7. Explain why $^{40}_{20}$Ca and $^{40}_{19}$K are not considered isotopes even though they have the same atomic masses.

   _____

   _____

8. Explain how the following can both be correct electron configurations for aluminum, which has 13 electrons: $1s^2 2s^2 2p^6 3s^2 3p^1$ and $1s^2 2s^2 2p^5 3s^2 3p^2$.

   _____

   _____

UNIT 2

Parts of an Atom

An atomic symbol may include the mass number as a superscript and the atomic number as a subscript. The atomic number represents the number of protons and therefore the number of electrons. The mass number represents the number of protons and neutrons.

Complete the following table.

Atomic Symbol	Number of Protons	Number of Neutrons	Number of Electrons
$^{4}_{2}He$	_____	_____	_____
$^{80}_{35}Br$	_____	_____	_____
^{11}B	5	_____	_____
$_{55}Cs$	_____	78	_____
Pd	46	60	_____

1. An atom of gold (Au) has 79 protons and 118 neutrons. Write the atomic symbol for this atom.

_____

2. A lead atom has the atomic symbol $^{207}_{82}Pb$. How many neutrons does this atom have in its nucleus?

_____

3. How many electrons are present in an atom with an atomic number of 13 and a mass number of 27?

_____

4. What is the mass number of an atom that has 29 electrons, 29 protons, and 35 neutrons? _____

5. An atom of neon (Ne) gas has 10 electrons and a mass number of 21. Write the atomic symbol for this atom. _____

UNIT 2 — Isotopes and Atomic Masses

> *Isotopes have the same atomic number but different mass numbers. Therefore, isotopes have the same number of protons but different number of neutrons. The average atomic mass of an element is a weighted average of all the atomic masses of the isotopes of that element.*

1. Four isotopes of lead include lead-204, lead-206, lead-207, and lead-208. The average atomic mass of a lead atom is 207.2 amu. Which isotope of lead is likely to be the most abundant? _____

2. What do all isotopes of an element have in common?

_____

_____

3. What additional information must you have to determine how many neutrons are present in a silver-108 atom?

_____

_____

4. Explain why carbon-14 and nitrogen-14 are not considered isotopes.

_____

_____

5. Explain why oxygen-16 and $^{16}_{8}O$ are not considered isotopes.

_____

_____

6. Complete the following table for three isotopes of the element barium (Ba).

Atomic Symbol	# of Protons	# of Neutrons	# of Electrons
$^{130}_{56}Ba$	_____	_____	_____
Ba		81	
^{140}Ba	_____	_____	_____

7. Write the atomic symbol for two isotopes of uranium (U), whose atomic number is 92. One isotope has 142 neutrons, and the other isotope has 146 neutrons. _____

8. Calculate the average atomic mass of the element iron (Fe) from the following table.

isotope	relative abundance
iron-54	6%
iron-56	92%
iron-57	2%

UNIT 2  Electron Configuration Puzzle

Use the clues to unscramble the letters to form a word. Then, unscramble all the circled letters to get the answer to the question.

1. toam—made of protons, neutrons, and electrons

Ⓞ __ __ Ⓞ

2. tibor—what electrons do in their travels

__ __ __ Ⓞ Ⓞ

3. gerney—what electrons have as they travel

Ⓞ __ Ⓞ __ __ __

4. rundog—the state in which an electron is the lowest available energy level

__ __ Ⓞ __ __ __

5. rohdengy—the element that has only one electron

__ __ Ⓞ __ __ __ __ __

6. hipcersal—the shape of an *s* orbital

Ⓞ __ __ __ __ Ⓞ Ⓞ __ __

7. centlelex—what someone might say about your knowledge of atoms

__ Ⓞ __ __ __ __ __ __ __

8. What an electron might say when it moves to a higher energy level

__ __ __ __ __ __ __ __ __ __ __ __ __ __!

UNIT 2 Writing Electron Configurations

Write the electron configuration for the following atoms. The illustration below shows the energy levels of various orbitals. Assume that all electrons are in the ground state unless otherwise noted.

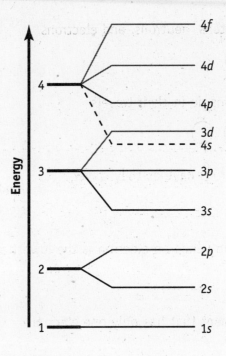

1. an atom with 7 electrons

_____

2. an atom that has 10 protons in its nucleus

_____

3. $^{23}_{11}$Na

_____

4. a hydrogen atom that has one excited electron in the 3p orbital

_____

5. $^{40}_{20}$Ca

_____

6. $^{40}_{20}$Ca in an excited state where one electron has jumped from the 2p orbital to the 4p orbital

_____

UNIT 2   The Periodic Table

Write the letter of the definition or description on the right in front of the appropriate term on the left.

_____ 1. ionization energy

_____ 2. group

_____ 3. atomic number

_____ 4. valence electron

_____ 5. period

_____ 6. nonmetal

_____ 7. alkali metal

_____ 8. noble gas

_____ 9. electronegativity

_____ 10. semiconductor

a. horizontal row

b. metalloid

c. located on the right side of a periodic table

d. what is needed to remove an electron from an atom

e. unreactive

f. Group 1 element

g. basis for arrangement of a periodic table

h. located in the outermost energy level

i. ability of an atom to attract an electron

j. vertical row

NAME _____   DATE _____

UNIT 2  Ionization Energy: A Periodic Trend

> *Ionization energy is the energy required to remove an electron from an atom.*

Use the graph below to answer the following questions.

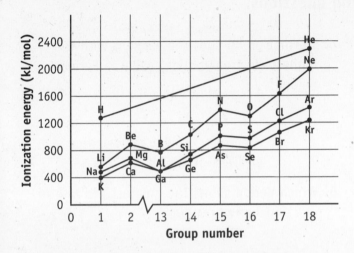

5. What is unusual about the ionization energies for Groups 13 and 16?

_____

_____

_____

_____

_____

1. Which element has the lowest ionization energy? the highest ionization energy?

_____

_____

6. Can members of different groups have the same ionization energies? Explain your answer.

_____

_____

_____

2. Which two elements have the same ionization energies?

_____

_____

7. Which group has the lowest ionization energy values?

_____

_____

3. Explain how this graph illustrates a periodic trend.

_____

_____

8. How does the ionization energy of Ne compare to that of Se?

_____

_____

4. Which group has the highest ionization energies?

_____

_____

UNIT 2 Electronegativity: A Periodic Trend

> *Electronegativity is a measure of the ability of an atom in a chemical compound to attract electrons.*

Use the graph below to answer the following questions.

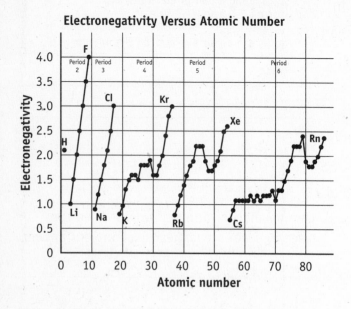

Electronegativity Versus Atomic Number

4. To what group does the element with the highest electronegativity value in Period 5 belong?

_____

_____

5. Which period shows the greatest increase in electronegativity values?

_____

_____

6. Which group of elements has the lowest electronegativity values?

_____

_____

1. Which element has the highest electronegativity value?

_____

2. Explain how this graph illustrates a periodic trend.

_____

_____

_____

7. As part of a chemical compound, which element consists of atoms that most strongly attract electrons of other atoms?

_____

_____

3. Which element in Period 3 has three times the electronegativity value compared to that of Li in Period 2?

_____

8. This graph plots electronegativity values versus atomic number. Draw a graph that would show electronegativity values versus the elements in Period 2.

Chemical Compounds

The elements of Group 18, the noble gases, exist as individual atoms. As a rule, elements in Groups 1–17 are not found as individual atoms in nature. Rather, their atoms are joined with other atoms as part of chemical compounds. The noble gases do not form compounds—at least not easily—because they have a complete set of electrons in their outermost energy level. A complete set means having two electrons in the first energy level or eight electrons in any of the other energy levels.

In contrast, elements in Groups 1–17 do not have complete sets of electrons in their outermost energy levels. A complete set of electrons results in stability. As a result, atoms that lack a complete set tend to react with similar atoms to achieve stability. There are several ways atoms can become stable.

Covalent Compounds

Some atoms combine to form a compound by sharing electrons. This results in a **covalent bond**, which is formed when atoms share one or more pairs of electrons. Consider what happens between a hydrogen atom and a fluorine atom. Hydrogen has one valence electron as shown by its electron configuration: $1s^1$. Notice that hydrogen's sole electron is also its valence electron and located in the first energy level. Recall that this energy level can hold a maximum of two electrons.

Fluorine has seven valence electrons as shown by its electron configuration: $1s^2 2s^2 2p^5$. Notice that fluorine's seven valence electrons are located in the second energy level, with two electrons in the $2s$ orbital and five electrons in the $2p$ orbital. Recall that the second energy level can hold a maximum of eight electrons.

Key Terms

covalent bond—a bond formed when atoms share one or more pairs of electrons

single covalent bond—a covalent bond between two atoms achieving stability by sharing a pair of electrons

polar covalent bond—a covalent bond in which a pair of electrons shared by two atoms is held more closely by one atom

nonpolar covalent bond—a covalent bond in which the bonding electrons are equally attracted to both bonded atoms

double covalent bond—a covalent bond formed by sharing two pairs of electrons

triple covalent bond—a covalent bond formed by sharing three pairs of electrons

structural formula—a formula that shows how the atoms are arranged or connected

ionic bond—a bond that forms when one atom gives up one or more electrons to another atom

cation—an ion that has given up an electron, producing a positive charge

anion—an ion that has accepted an electron, producing a negative charge

polyatomic ion—an ion formed when several atoms combine

Lewis structure—a structural formula in which electrons are represented by dots; dot pairs or dashes between two atomic symbols represent pairs in covalent bonds

By sharing a pair of electrons, hydrogen can have two electrons in its first energy level. Therefore, the hydrogen atom achieves stability. This shared pair of electrons also allows fluorine to have eight electrons in its second energy level. Like hydrogen, fluorine can also be stable. Hydrogen and fluorine have achieved stability by sharing a pair of electrons. This is known as a **single covalent bond** and is shown as a long dash drawn between the two atoms: H — F. This can also be written simply as HF.

A single covalent bond can also form between two hydrogen atoms: H — H. This can also be written as H_2. This covalent bond between the two hydrogen atoms allows each atom to have two electrons in its first energy level. Like H — F, H — H is also stable. However, there are two important differences between these two substances. First, H — F is a compound because two elements have been combined. In contrast, H — H is an element because it consists solely of bonded hydrogen atoms.

A second difference can be seen in the way H — F and H — H share electrons. With more protons in its nucleus, the F atom attracts the shared pair of electrons more than the H atom. Therefore, the sharing is unequal. This is known as a **polar covalent bond**. In contrast, the sharing of electrons in H — H is equal because both H atoms have one proton. The equal sharing of electrons between two atoms is known as a **nonpolar covalent bond**.

Atoms can form covalent bonds by sharing two pairs of electrons. Examples include O＝O and O＝C＝O. The first substance is oxygen gas, O_2, which is an element. The second substance is carbon dioxide gas, CO_2, which is a compound. The bonds in both O_2 and CO_2 are **double covalent bonds**.

Atoms can also form covalent bonds by sharing three pairs of electrons. Examples include N≡N, or N_2, and H — C≡C — H, or C_2H_2. The bonds between the two N atoms and the two C atoms are known as **triple covalent bonds**. With only one type of atom, N_2 is an element formed by a triple covalent bond. In contrast, C_2H_2 is a compound with a triple covalent bond between its two C atoms and single covalent bonds between the H and C atoms.

Both N≡N and H — C≡C — H are examples of **structural formulas**. A structural formula shows how the atoms are arranged or connected. Both N_2 and C_2H_2 are examples of chemical formulas, which show only the kinds and number of atoms present but not their arrangement.

Covalent compounds are named using a system of prefixes. For example, SO_2 is named sulfur dioxide, while SO_3 is named sulfur trioxide, and P_2S_5 is named diphosphorus pentasulfide.

Ionic Compounds

Not all atoms join by sharing electrons to form a covalent bond. Instead, some atoms give and take electrons to form a bond. A bond that forms when one atom gives up one or more electrons to another atom is called an **ionic bond**.

Consider how a bond forms between sodium (Na), which has the electron configuration $1s^2 2s^2 2p^6 3s^1$, and chlorine (Cl), which has the electron configuration, $1s^2 2s^2 2p^6 3s^2 3p^5$. Notice that Na has one valence electron, while Cl has seven valence electrons. By giving up its one valence electron, Na will have a complete set of electrons in its second energy level. In giving up an electron, sodium forms an ion. An ion is an atom that has gained or lost one or more electrons and has a negative or positive charge. Giving up an electron produces an ion that has a positive charge. A sodium ion is an example of a **cation** and is written as Na^+.

By accepting the one electron given up by the Na atom, the Cl atom will have a complete set of electrons in its third energy level. Accepting an electron produces an ion that has a negative charge. A chlorine ion is an example of an **anion** and is written as Cl^-.

A Na^+ cation and a Cl^- anion are attracted to one another because of their opposite charges. This attraction produces an ionic bond between the two ions. The formula for the compound they produce is written as NaCl and is called sodium chloride.

Ionic bonds form between ions of opposite charges. The compound the ions form is always neutral. Consider what happens when a calcium (Ca) atom forms an ion. With two valence electrons, Ca must lose both these electrons to achieve stability. Losing two electrons produces a Ca^{2+} cation. Two Cl^- anions are needed to form an ionic bond with a

Ca^{2+} cation to produce a neutral compound. Therefore, the formula is written as $CaCl_2$ and is called calcium chloride.

In some cases, several atoms combine to form a single ion. This ion is called a **polyatomic ion**. Examples include OH^-, CrO_4^{2-}, and NH_4^+. The formula for a polyatomic ion must be enclosed in parentheses when it is present more than once. For example, the formula for a compound made of Fe^{3+} ions and OH^- polyatomic ions is written as $Fe(OH)_3$. Three OH^- ions are needed to produce a neutral compound with one Fe^{3+} ion.

Electronegativity and Bond Types

Looking at the valence electrons of an atom can give you a clue as to what type of bond an atom will form. For example, an atom with only one valence electron is likely to lose that electron to form an ionic bond. However, there is another method to use to determine what type of bond will form between two atoms. This method involves differences in electronegativity values.

Recall that electronegativity is a value assigned to an atom in a chemical compound based on its ability to attract electrons. The electronegativity difference between two atoms can be used to determine the type of bond they form. If the electronegativity difference falls between 0 and 0.5, then the two atoms form a nonpolar covalent bond. If the difference falls between 0.5 and 2.1, then the two atoms form a polar covalent bond. A difference in electronegativity values between 2.1 and 3.3 results in an ionic bond.

For example, nitrogen (N) has an electronegativity value of 3.0, while that of oxygen (O) is 3.4. The difference between these two electronegativity values is 0.4, meaning that a bond that forms between N and O is a nonpolar covalent one. However, oxygen will form a polar covalent bond with carbon, which has an electronegativity value of 2.6 ($3.4 - 2.6 = 0.8$). Oxygen will also form a polar covalent bond with boron, which has an electronegativity value of 2.0 ($3.4 - 2.0 = 1.4$). The greater the difference in electronegativity values, the greater the polarity of the bond. Therefore, the degree of polarity in the bond between O and B (difference of 1.4) is greater than the degree of polarity in the bond between O and C (difference of 0.8).

Oxygen forms an ionic bond with calcium because the difference in their electronegativity values is 2.4. You should keep in mind that there are no distinct boundaries between the bond types. The distinction between nonpolar covalent, polar covalent, and ionic bonds based on differences in electronegativity values is arbitrary. Nonetheless, the distinction is useful in predicting the properties of a compound.

Lewis Structures

In 1920, an American chemist named G. N. Lewis developed a simple system to show the valence electrons of an atom. This system uses an element's symbol to represent the nucleus and the electrons, if any, of the inner energy levels. One or more dots are used to represent the atom's valence electrons. This system is known as an electron-dot diagram or a **Lewis structure**. For example, the Lewis structure for hydrogen is drawn as follows.

H·

Notice that hydrogen's lone valence electron is represented by a dot, while its symbol represents its nucleus.

The Lewis structure for chlorine, which has seven valence electrons, is drawn as follows.

:Cl·

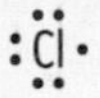

When drawing a Lewis structure, the dots must be placed around the symbol so that each side contains a dot before any side can contain a pair of dots. For example, the Lewis structure for carbon, with four valence electrons, is drawn as follows.

·C·

A Lewis structure can then be used to draw atoms that combine by forming a covalent bond. For example, consider the Lewis structure for two covalently-bonded hydrogen atoms that is drawn as follows.

H:H

This Lewis structure represents hydrogen gas made of two hydrogen atoms that share a pair of electrons. A pair of electrons that is shared by two atoms can also be shown by a long dash.

H—H

The following is the Lewis structure for two chlorine atoms that form a single covalent bond.

:Cl:Cl:

Notice that each chlorine atom in the above Lewis structure has three unshared pairs of electrons. Each chlorine atom also has one shared pair of electrons that represent the single covalent bond.

Lewis structures can show how a hydrogen atom and chlorine atom form a single covalent bond.

H· + ·Cl: ⟶ H—Cl:

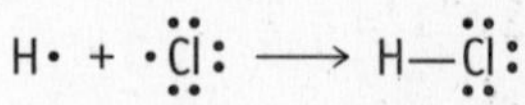

Notice that the hydrogen atom has one shared pair of electrons, while the chlorine atom has three unshared pairs and one shared pair. Compounds that contain double and triple bonds can also be drawn as Lewis structures.

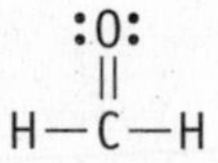

:O:
‖
H—C—H   N≡N

UNIT 3

Review

Darken the circle by the best answer.

1. The unequal sharing of two pairs of electrons is known as a
   - (A) single, polar covalent bond.
   - (B) double, polar covalent bond.
   - (C) single, nonpolar covalent bond.
   - (D) double, nonpolar covalent bond.

2. The chemical name for water, H_2O, is
   - (A) hydrogen oxide.
   - (B) hydrogen dioxide.
   - (C) dihydrogen oxide.
   - (D) dihydrogen dioxide.

3. An atom that loses an electron is called a(n)
   - (A) cation.
   - (B) anion.
   - (C) polyatomic ion.
   - (D) ionic compound.

4. Which represents the formula for the ionic compound that forms between Ca^{2+} and PO_4^{3-}?
   - (A) $CaPO_4$
   - (B) $Ca_3\ PO_4$
   - (C) $Ca(PO_4)_2$
   - (D) $Ca_3(PO_4)_2$

5. If the electrons are shared unequally between two atoms, then the bond formed is
   - (A) nonpolar covalent.
   - (B) polar covalent.
   - (C) ionic.
   - (D) either nonpolar covalent or polar covalent.

6. The electronegativity value of S is 2.6, while that of O is 3.4. What type of bond do these two atoms form?
   - (A) nonpolar covalent
   - (B) polar covalent
   - (C) ionic
   - (D) either nonpolar covalent or polar covalent

7. In a Lewis structure, a long dash represents
   - (A) the nucleus of an atom.
   - (B) the inner electrons.
   - (C) a shared pair of electrons.
   - (D) an unshared pair of electrons.

8. Write the formulas for titanium(III) sulfate, which is used as a stain remover, and for chromium(III) phosphate, a green pigment.

   _____

9. In a Lewis structure, what does a chemical symbol, such as Ne, represent?

   _____

   _____

UNIT 3

Covalent Bonds

> *A covalent bond is a bond formed when atoms share one or more pairs of electrons.*

Draw the structural formula for each of the following combinations of atoms. Check a periodic table to determine how many valence electrons each atom must share to achieve a complete set in its outermost energy level.

1. Cl and Cl

_____

2. H and Cl

_____

3. H and two Os

_____

4. C and four Hs

_____

5. N and three Hs

6. C and two Ss

_____

7. O and two Cls

_____

8. H, O, and Cl

_____

9. two Cs and four Hs

_____

10. C, two Cls, and two Fs

Unit 3, Chemical Compounds
Chemistry, SV 0424-7

UNIT 3

Names of Covalent Compounds

Based on their names, draw the structural formulas for each of the following compounds. The prefix indicates the number of atoms present for that element.

1. hydrogen bromide

_____

2. nitrogen triflouride

_____

3. iodine chloride

_____

4. dichlorine oxide

_____

5. carbon disulfide

Based on their names, write the chemical formulas for each of the following compounds.

6. phosphorus trichloride

_____

7. dinitrogen oxide

_____

8. xenon tetrafluoride

_____

9. trisilicon tetranitride

_____

10. trineptunium octoxide

_____

UNIT 3

Ionic Compounds

Write the formulas for the ionic compounds that form between the following elements. Check a periodic table to determine how many valence electrons each atom must lose or gain to determine the ion that it forms. Be sure that each formula you write represents a neutral compound.

1. K and Br

   _____

2. Mg and Br

   _____

3. Ca and O

   _____

4. Na and O

   _____

5. K and N

   _____

6. Al and Br

   _____

7. Ba and S

   _____

8. Al and S

   _____

9. Li and O

   _____

10. Al and O

    _____

UNIT 3

Polyatomic Ions

> *A polyatomic ion is an ion formed when several atoms combine.*

Use the following table to write the formulas of compounds that contain polyatomic ions. Be sure that each compound is neutral with a balance of charges between the cations and anions. Enclose any polyatomic ion in parentheses if it is present more than once in a compound.

1. sodium acetate _____

2. calcium hydroxide _____

3. aluminum phosphate _____

4. ammonium sulfate _____

5. lithium thiosulfate _____

6. ammonium hydroxide _____

7. aluminum carbonate _____

8. potassium nitrate _____

9. magnesium nitrite _____

10. sodium peroxide _____

Ion Name	Formula
Acetate	CH_3COO^-
Ammonium	NH_4^+
Carbonate	CO_3^{2-}
Chromate	CrO_4^{2-}
Cyanide	CN^-
Dichromate	$Cr_2O_7^{2-}$
Hydroxide	OH^-
Nitrate	NO_3^-
Nitrite	NO_2^-
Permanganate	MnO_4^-
Peroxide	O_2^{2-}
Phosphate	PO_4^{3-}
Sulfate	SO_4^{2-}
Sulfite	SO_3^{2-}
Thiosulfate	$S_2O_3^{2-}$

Unit 3, Chemical Compounds
Chemistry, SV 0424-7

UNIT 3

Stable Ions

Not all atoms form ions that have a complete set of electrons in their outermost energy levels. For example, a copper atom may give up one electron to form a Cu^+ cation. A copper atom may also give up two electrons to form a Cu^{2+} cation. Both the Cu^+ and Cu^{2+} cations are stable even though they do not have a complete set of electrons in their outermost energy levels. To distinguish between these two cations, Cu^+ is written as the copper(I) ion, and Cu^{2+} is written as the copper(II) ion. Therefore, the formula for copper(I) chloride is CuCl, while the formula for copper(II) chloride is $CuCl_2$.

Use the table at right to write the formulas for the following compounds.

Group 6	Group 7	Group 8	Group 9	Group 10	Group 11
Cr^{2+}	Mn^{2+}	Fe^{2+}	Co^{2+}	Ni^{2+}	Cu^+
Cr^{3+}	Mn^{3+}	Fe^{3+}	Co^{3+}		Cu^{2+}

1. iron(III) hydroxide _____

2. chromium(II) bromide _____

3. copper(II) phosphate _____

4. cobalt(III) sulfate _____

5. cobalt(II) sulfate _____

6. manganese(II) oxide _____

7. copper(I) carbonate _____

8. chromium(III) acetate _____

9. copper(I) cyanide _____

10. nickel sulfate _____

UNIT 3

Determining Bond Type

Use the following table of electronegativity values to determine what type of bond the two atoms will form.

H
2.2

Li	Be
1.0	1.6

Na	Mg
0.9	1.3

B	C	N	O	F
2.0	2.6	3.0	3.4	4.0

Al	Si	P	S	Cl
1.6	1.9	2.2	2.6	3.2

K	Ca	Sc	Ti	V	Cr	Mn	Fe	Co	Ni	Cu	Zn	Ga	Ge	As	Se	Br
0.8	1.0	1.4	1.5	1.6	1.7	1.6	1.9	1.9	1.9	2.0	1.7	1.8	2.0	2.2	2.5	3.0

Rb	Sr	Y	Zr	Nb	Mo	Tc	Ru	Rh	Pd	Ag	Cd	In	Sn	Sb	Te	I
0.8	1.0	1.2	1.3	1.6	2.2	1.9	2.2	2.3	2.2	1.9	1.7	1.8	1.9	2.0	2.1	2.7

Cs	Ba	La	Hf	Ta	W	Re	Os	Ir	Pt	Au	Hg	Tl	Pb	Bi	Po	At
0.8	0.9	1.1	1.3	1.5	2.4	1.9	2.2	2.2	2.3	2.5	2.0	1.8	2.1	2.0	2.0	2.2

Fr	Ra	Ac
0.7	0.9	1.1

1. Cr and O _____

2. Sr and O _____

3. Cl and Br _____

4. H and F _____

5. Ca and Cl _____

6. Ca and C _____

7. Pb and H _____

8. Br and Br _____

9. Mg and F _____

10. Na and Br _____

Unit 3, Chemical Compounds
Chemistry, SV 0424-7

UNIT 3

Lewis Structures

> *A Lewis Structure is a structural formula in which electrons are represented as dots. Dot pairs or dashes between two atomic symbols represent pairs in covalent bonds.*

Draw the Lewis structure for each of the following atoms. A Lewis structure includes the atomic symbol surrounded by dots which represent the valence electrons.

1. calcium

2. iodine

3. oxygen

4. neon

5. boron

Draw the Lewis structure for each of the following compounds. Be sure to indicate a covalent bond by a long dash.

6. ClF

7. HOCl

8. NF_3

9. CS_2

10. CH_3OH

UNIT 3 Chemical Compound Crossword

Across

1. symbol for a shared pair of electrons
5. bond formed by unequal sharing of electrons
6. electron sharing between two identical atoms
7. type of bond formed between Na and Cl
9. ability of an atom in a compound to attract an electron
12. covalent bond formed between two O atoms
13. symbols for elements in dinitrogen oxide
14. smallest unit of an element
16. what atoms become when they lose or gain an electron
17. the electronegativity difference between two identical atoms
19. scientist who developed way of showing valence electrons
21. number of electrons that form a single covalent bond
22. symbol used for a valence electron

Down

2. what an atom becomes when it has a complete set of electrons
3. part of atom that forms a bond
4. ion with a negative charge
8. ion with a positive charge
9. a substance that cannot be separated or broken down into simpler substances by ordinary means
10. maximum number of electrons in the first energy level
11. equal sharing results in this type of bond
15. type of bond three pairs of electrons form
18. maximum number of electrons in the second energy level
20. what electrons do in a covalent bond

Unit 3, Chemical Compounds
Chemistry, SV 0424-7

A **chemical reaction** is the process by which one or more substances change into one or more new substances. The chemical and physical properties of the new substances are different from those of the original substances. The original substances, which can be either elements or compounds, are known as the reactants. The new substances are called products. During a chemical reaction, the atoms in the reactants are only rearranged. Atoms are neither created nor destroyed. As a result, the total mass of the products equals the total mass of the reactants. This is known as the **law of conservation of mass**. Any equation that describes a chemical reaction must be balanced so that it obeys the law of conservation of mass.

Balancing Equations

An equation is balanced when the number of atoms for each element is the same on both the reactants' side and the products' side. For example, consider what happens when someone uses a gas barbecue. The tank contains a gas called propane, C_3H_8, which burns in oxygen, O_2, to produce carbon dioxide, CO_2, and water vapor, H_2O. The equation for this reaction is written as follows.

$$C_3H_8 + O_2 \rightarrow CO_2 + H_2O$$

Notice that the above equation is not balanced. For example, there are 3 C atoms on the reactants' side, but only 1 C atom on the products' side. This suggests that two carbon atoms have been destroyed, which is a violation of the law of conservation of mass. To obey this law and balance

Key Terms

chemical reaction—the process by which one or more substances change into one or more new substances

law of conservation of mass—a law that states that the total mass of the products equals the total mass of the reactants

combustion reaction—a reaction involving a carbon-based compound reacting with oxygen

decomposition reaction—a reaction where a single compound breaks down into two or more elements or simpler compounds

synthesis reaction—a reaction where two or more substances combine to form a new compound

single-displacement reaction—a reaction where a single element reacts with a compound and displaces another element from the compound

double-displacement reaction—a reaction where two compounds appear to exchange ions and form two new compounds

law of conservation of energy—a law that states that energy can only be transformed from one form to another, not created or destroyed

activation energy—the minimum energy required to start a chemical reaction

activated complex—a molecule in an unstable state intermediate to the reactants and the products in the chemical reaction

polyatomic ions. For example, consider the following unbalanced equation.

$$HgCl_2 + AgNO_3 \rightarrow Hg(NO_3)_2 + AgCl$$

Notice that there are two nitrate polyatomic ions, NO_3, on the product side and only one NO_3 polyatomic ion on the reactant side. The best way to balance this equation is by placing a 2 in front of $AgNO_3$ and in front of $AgCl$ so that the balanced equation is written as follows.

$$HgCl_2 + 2AgNO_3 \rightarrow Hg(NO_3)_2 + 2AgCl$$

Types of Chemical Reactions

To make it easier to study and understand chemical reactions, it is helpful to classify them into several types. In this way, you can more easily predict the products that will form. Classifying reactions can also help you balance the equation more easily. The following are some major types of chemical reactions. Keep in mind that these are not the only ones and that some reactions do not fit into any of these or other types.

One type of chemical reaction is known as a **combustion reaction**, which involves the reaction of a carbon-based compound with oxygen. The products are carbon dioxide and water vapor. Energy as heat is also released. An example of a combustion reaction is shown by the following balanced equation.

$$CH_3CH_2OH + 3O_2 \rightarrow 2CO_2 + 3H_2O + \text{energy as heat}$$

Another type of reaction is known as a **decomposition reaction** where a single compound breaks down into two or more elements or simpler compounds. Decomposition reactions often involve an input of energy. An example is the decomposition of calcium carbonate.

$$CaCO_3 + \text{energy as heat} \rightarrow CaO + CO_2$$

A **synthesis reaction** involves two or more substances combining to form a new compound. Any reaction in which only one product is formed is a synthesis reaction, as shown by the following equation.

$$CO_2 + H_2O \rightarrow H_2CO_3$$

the carbon atoms, a coefficient is placed in front of a formula. Therefore, the equation is rewritten as follows.

$$C_3H_8 + O_2 \rightarrow 3CO_2 + H_2O$$

Notice that there are now 3 C atoms on both sides of the equation. However, this equation still suggests that hydrogen atoms have been destroyed because there are 8 H atoms on the reactants' side and only 2 H atoms on the products' side. Therefore, the above equation must be rewritten as follows.

$$C_3H_8 + O_2 \rightarrow 3CO_2 + 4H_2O$$

The above equation still violates the law of conservation of mass because oxygen atoms appear to have been created. Notice that there are 10 O atoms on the products' side and only 2 O atoms on the reactants' side. Therefore, the above equation must be rewritten as follows.

$$C_3H_8 + 5O_2 \rightarrow 3CO_2 + 4H_2O$$

The above equation is balanced because the numbers of atoms for each element are equal on both sides of the equation. Notice that the only way to balance an equation is with the use of coefficients. Notice also that 1 is never written as a coefficient. The subscripts in a formula are never changed once the formula is correctly written. Keep in mind that a coefficient, however, can be changed any number of times until the equation is completely balanced.

The best way to balance a chemical equation does not always involve balancing the individual atoms one at a time. This is especially true when dealing with

In a **single-displacement reaction**, a single element reacts with a compound and displaces another element from the compound. The following equation illustrates a single displacement reaction.

$$2Al + 3CuCl_2 \rightarrow 2AlCl_3 + 3Cu$$

A **double-displacement reaction** occurs when two compounds appear to exchange ions and form two new compounds. Notice how the two compounds in the following reaction appear to switch ions.

$$2AgNO_3 + K_2SO_4 \rightarrow Ag_2SO_4 + 2KNO_3$$

Energy Changes

All chemical reactions are accompanied by changes in energy. Reactions in which energy is released, usually as light or heat energy, are known as *exothermic reactions*. Reactions in which energy is absorbed are known as *endothermic reactions*. Keep in mind that energy is neither created nor destroyed in both exothermic and endothermic reactions. According to the **law of conservation of energy**, energy can only be transformed from one form to another. For example, an exothermic reaction may transform chemical energy into light energy. This transformation of energy occurs when you activate a light stick, changing chemical energy into light energy.

Exothermic and endothermic reactions do have something in common. Both require a minimum quantity of energy before the chemical reaction can occur. The minimum energy required to start a chemical reaction is known as the **activation energy**. For example, the following graph illustrates changes in energy as the decomposition of HI proceeds.

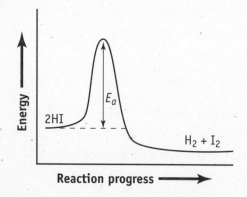

Notice that the activation energy is represented by the symbol, E_a. The highest point on the graph represents the **activated complex**, where the reactant has sufficient energy for the reaction to proceed. Notice that the products of the reaction, H_2 and I_2, have a lower energy level than the reactant, HI. Therefore, the decomposition of HI is an exothermic reaction in which energy is released. Contrast this reaction to the decomposition of HBr as shown in the following graph.

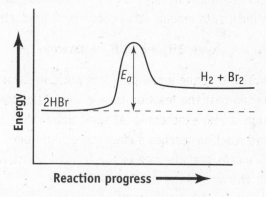

Notice that the products, H_2 and Br_2, have a higher energy level than the reactant, HBr. This increase in energy level represents an endothermic reaction. Notice also that activation energy is again required before the reaction can proceed. The decomposition of HBr occurs at a faster rate than the decomposition of HI because the decomposition of HBr has a lower activation energy.

A catalyst is often added to a reaction to speed up the reaction. Catalysts affect the rate of a reaction by lowering the activation energy. The following graph illustrates how three catalysts, iodide, MnO_2, and catalase, affect the rate of a reaction in which H_2O_2 decomposes.

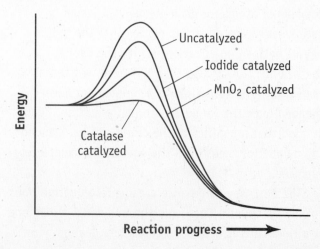

Chemical Equilibrium

Many reactions proceed in only one direction—from reactants to products. Such reactions are called completion reactions. However, in other reactions, the products can reform the reactants. Such reactions are called reversible reactions. The following is an example of a commercially-valuable, reversible reaction, which involves the synthesis of ammonia from nitrogen and hydrogen. Ammonia is used to make fertilizers, among other commercial products.

$$N_2 + 3H_2 \leftrightarrow 2NH_3 + \text{energy}$$

Notice that the arrow points in both directions, indicating that the reaction is reversible. The forward reaction is also exothermic. At some point, the forward reaction reaches a chemical equilibrium, which means that the rate of the forward reaction equals the rate of the reverse reaction.

A French chemist named Henri Le Châtelier developed a principle to explain what happens to equilibrium reactions when they are disturbed or stressed. Chemical equilibria respond to three kinds of stress: changes in temperature, changes in pressure, and changes in concentrations of reactants or products. A chemical equilibrium will respond so that the stress is alleviated until the rates of the forward and reverse reactions are again equal.

For example, suppose more N_2 or H_2 are added to the above reaction mixture. This change will create a stress by increasing the concentrations of the reactants. As a result, Le Châtelier's principle states that the above equilibrium will shift toward the right to reduce this stress. Similarly, increasing the concentration of NH_3 would shift the equilibrium to the left. Increasing the temperature would shift the equilibrium to the left. Increasing the pressure would shift the equilibrium to the right because it would favor the smaller volume. In other words, increasing the pressure would favor an increase in the concentration of NH_3 and a decrease in the concentrations of N_2 and H_2.

UNIT 4

Review

Darken the circle by the best answer.

1. To balance a chemical equation, you may adjust the

- Ⓐ formulas.
- Ⓑ coefficients.
- Ⓒ number of reactants.
- Ⓓ subscripts.

2. Examine the following unbalanced equation.

$$Al + Fe_2O_3 \rightarrow Fe + Al_2O_3$$

When the above equation is correctly balanced, what is the coefficient in front of Fe?

- Ⓐ 1
- Ⓑ 2
- Ⓒ 3
- Ⓓ 4

3. The reaction type that has only one reactant is

- Ⓐ decomposition.
- Ⓑ synthesis.
- Ⓒ combustion.
- Ⓓ double-displacement.

4. The reaction type that has only one product is

- Ⓐ combustion.
- Ⓑ single-replacement.
- Ⓒ decomposition.
- Ⓓ synthesis.

5. In a graph that shows how energy changes as a chemical reaction proceeds, the activated complex appears at the

- Ⓐ left end of the curve.
- Ⓑ right end of the curve.
- Ⓒ peak of the curve.
- Ⓓ bottom of the curve.

6. In an exothermic reaction, the products have

- Ⓐ a higher energy level than the reactants.
- Ⓑ a lower energy level than the reactants.
- Ⓒ the same energy level as the reactants.
- Ⓓ the highest energy level at any point during the reaction.

7. A chemical reaction is in equilibrium when

- Ⓐ no reactants remain.
- Ⓑ forward and reverse reactions have ceased.
- Ⓒ forward and reverse reaction rates are equal.
- Ⓓ as much product as possible has formed.

8. Write the balanced equation for the reaction that occurs between ethanol, C_2H_5OH, and oxygen to produce carbon dioxide and water.

_____

9. The reaction in question 8 is exothermic. How does the energy level of ethanol compare to the energy level of carbon dioxide?

_____

_____

_____

UNIT 4

Balancing Equations

Balance the following equations so that each one obeys the law of conservation of mass. Place coefficients where they are needed to balance the equation.

1. reaction between sodium and chlorine gas to produce sodium chloride, or table salt

$$Na + Cl_2 \rightarrow NaCl$$

2. breakdown of sodium azide, which helps inflate a car's airbag

$$NaN_3 \rightarrow Na + N_2$$

3. production of ozone gas by a car's exhaust

$$NO_2 + O_2 \rightarrow NO + O_3$$

4. removal of carbon dioxide to purify the air for an astronaut in a spacecraft

$$LiOH + CO_2 \rightarrow Li_2CO_3 + H_2O$$

5. production of ammonia for making fertilizers

$$N_2 + H_2 \rightarrow NH_3$$

6. combustion of methane in a Bunsen burner

$$CH_4 + O_2 \rightarrow CO_2 + H_2O$$

7. production of zinc oxide, a white paste used to prevent sunburn

$$ZnS + O_2 \rightarrow ZnO + SO_2$$

8. combustion of gasoline (octane) in an automobile engine

$$C_8H_{18} + O_2 \rightarrow CO_2 + H_2O$$

9. production of silicon for use in computer chips

$$SiCl_4 + Mg \rightarrow MgCl_2 + Si$$

10. combining carbon monoxide and hydrogen gases to make methyl alcohol, a fuel used in race cars

$$CO + H_2 \rightarrow CH_3OH$$

11. production of aluminum sulfate, used in fire-retardant fabrics

$$Al_2O_3 + H_2SO_4 \rightarrow Al_2(SO_4)_3 + H_2O$$

12. production of copper nitrate, used to give a dark finish to copper objects

$$Cu + HNO_3 \rightarrow Cu(NO_3)_2 + H_2O + NO$$

UNIT 4
Translating Word Equations

First, write the word equation for each of the following reactions. Next, write the correct formula for each reactant and product. Finally, use coefficients to balance the chemical equation so that the law of conservation of mass is obeyed.

1. Nickel reacts with lead nitrate to produce nickel nitrate and lead.

2. Aluminum iodide and nickel are produced when aluminum and nickel(II) iodide react.

3. Water decomposes to form hydrogen and oxygen gases.

4. Sodium phosphate reacts with calcium nitrate to produce sodium nitrate and calcium phosphate.

5. Nitrogen monoxide and water vapor are produced from a reaction between ammonia and oxygen.

6. Iron(II) hydroxide reacts with hydrogen peroxide to produce iron(III) hydroxide.

Unit 4, Chemical Reactions
Chemistry, SV 0424-7

UNIT 4

Types of Chemical Reactions

> *A chemical reaction is the process by which one or more substances change into one or more new substances.*

Write the balanced equation for each of the following reactions. Also identify the type of reaction that the equation represents. The possible types of reactions include combustion, synthesis, decomposition, single-replacement, and double-replacement reactions.

1. Sodium reacts with iron(III) oxide to produce sodium oxide and iron.

_____

_____

2. Hydrogen bromide forms from hydrogen and bromine.

_____

_____

3. Metallic silver and chlorine gas form from silver chloride.

_____

_____

4. Carbon dioxide and water are produced when ethane, C_2H_6, reacts with oxygen.

_____

_____

5. Calcium oxide reacts with water to form calcium hydroxide.

_____

_____

6. Calcium hydroxide and hydrochloric acid (hydrogen chloride) produce calcium chloride and water.

_____

_____

7. Iron(III) nitrate reacts with lithium hydroxide to produce lithium nitrate and iron(III) hydroxide.

_____

_____

8. Iron and oxygen produce iron(III) oxide.

_____

_____

9. Carbon dioxide and water are produced when sucrose, $C_{12}H_{22}O_{11}$, reacts with oxygen.

_____

_____

UNIT 4 — Predicting the Products

Predict the products that will form in each of the following reactions. Identifying the type of reaction will help you predict the products. Then write both the word equation and the balanced equation for each reaction.

1. Hydrogen iodide breaks down.

2. Aluminum combines with oxygen.

3. Sodium bromide and chlorine react.

4. Butane, C_5H_{10}, reacts with oxygen.

5. Zinc is placed in a solution of copper(II) sulfate.

6. Barium chlorate decomposes. Hint: One product is oxygen.

7. Copper(II) sulfate reacts with ammonium sulfide.

8. Oxygen and methanol, CH_3OH, react.

9. Water decomposes.

10. Magnesium and nitrogen combine.

UNIT 4

Energy Changes I

Examine the following graph, which illustrates the energy changes that occur during a chemical reaction. Use the graph to answer the questions.

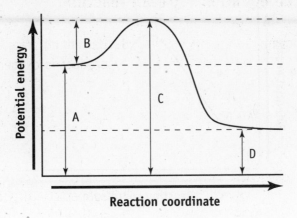

Reaction coordinate

1. What does arrow A represent?

_____

_____

2. What does arrow B represent?

_____

_____

3. What does arrow C represent?

_____

_____

4. What does arrow D represent?

_____

_____

5. Is this an example of an endothermic reaction or an exothermic reaction? Explain your choice.

_____

_____

_____

6. How can the highest potential energy level shown on this graph be lowered?

_____

_____

UNIT 4

Energy Changes II

Examine the following graph, which illustrates the energy changes that occur during a chemical reaction. Use the graph to answer the questions.

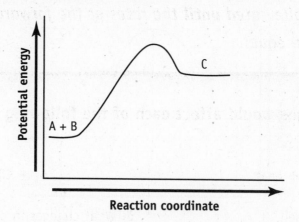

1. Does this diagram illustrate an exothermic reaction or an endothermic reaction? Explain your answer.

   _____

   _____

   _____

   _____

   _____

   _____

2. Place an X where the activated complex forms.

3. Draw a dashed line on the graph to show how a catalyst would affect this reaction.

4. Draw an arrow labeled Y to show the potential energy level of the reactants.

5. Draw an arrow labeled Z that represents the change in potential energy of this reaction.

UNIT 4

Chemical Equilibrium

> *LeChâtelier's principle states that a chemical equilibrium will respond so that the stress is alleviated until the rates of the forward and reverse reactions are again equal.*

Describe how the changes would affect each of the following chemical equilibria involving gases.

$$2NO_2 \leftrightarrow N_2O_4 + heat$$

1. The temperature is increased.

_____

_____

2. The pressure is decreased.

_____

_____

3. The concentration of NO_2 is increased.

_____

_____

4. The concentration of N_2O_4 is decreased.

_____

_____

5. The temperature is changed from 298 K to 264 K.

_____

$$H_2 + CO_2 \leftrightarrow H_2O + CO$$

6. What changes in concentrations of the products can be made to shift the equilibrium to the right?

_____

_____

_____

7. How would an increase in pressure affect this equilibrium? Explain your answer.

_____

_____

_____

_____

8. How would an increase in temperature affect this equilibrium?

_____

_____

_____

UNIT 5 — The Mole and Stoichiometry

Chemistry is a quantitative science, which means that it usually involves measurements and the recording of observations in numerical terms. The branch of chemistry that deals with quantities of substances involved in chemical reactions is known as **stoichiometry**. The key unit in stoichiometry is the **mole**. A mole is defined as the number of atoms of carbon in exactly 12 grams of carbon-12. The mole is used to calculate various values in chemistry, including the molar or gram-formula mass of a substance.

Molar Mass

The molar mass of a substance is used to convert between moles and grams. The molar mass of an element is the mass in grams of one mole of the element. Molar mass has the units grams per mol (g/mol). The molar mass of an element is numerically equal to the element's atomic mass from a periodic table. For example, a periodic table lists the mass of copper as 63.55 amu. Therefore, the molar mass of Cu is 63.55 g/mol. This information can be used to determine the mass in grams of 3.5 mol of Cu.

$$3.5 \ \text{mol Cu} \times \frac{63.55 \ \text{g Cu}}{1 \ \text{mol Cu}} = ?\text{g Cu} = 222 \ \text{g Cu}$$

The molar mass of a compound is calculated using the formula for the compound. For example, suppose you wanted to calculate the molar mass of barium nitrate. The formula for barium nitrate is $Ba(NO_3)_2$. First, find the number of moles of each element in this compound: 1 mol Ba, 2 mol N, and 6 mol O. Next, use a periodic table to find the molar mass of each element. The molar mass of Ba = 137.33 g/mol, N = 14.01 g/mol, and O = 16.00 g/mol. Finally, multiply the molar mass of each element by the number of moles of each element.

Key Terms

stoichiometry—the proportional relationships between two or more substances during a chemical reaction

mole—the number of atoms of carbon in exactly 12 grams of carbon-12

Avogadro's number—the value associated with the number of atoms of carbon in exactly one mole of carbon-12 (6.02×10^{23} units/mol)

percentage composition—the percentage by mass of each element in a compound

empirical formula—a chemical formula that shows the composition of a compound in terms of the relative numbers and kinds of atoms in the simplest ratio

molecular formula—a chemical formula that shows the number and kinds of atoms in a molecule, but not the arrangement of the atoms

solute—a substance that is dissolved

solvent—the substance in which the solute is dissolved

molarity—the concentration unit of a solution expressed as moles of solute dissolved per liter of solution

ideal gas law—a law which relates all four gas variables, including pressure, volume, and the number of moles of a gas, written as $PV = nRT$

effusion—the passage of a gas under pressure through a tiny opening

1 mol Ba (137.33 g/mol) + 2 mol N (28.02 g/mol) + 6 mol O (96.00 g/mol) = the molar mass of Ba(NO$_3$)$_2$ or 261.35 g/mol

You can use the molar mass of a substance to convert mass to moles. For example, you can calculate how many moles are present in 109.8 g Ba(NO$_3$)$_2$.

$$109.8 \text{ g Ba(NO}_3)_2 \times \frac{1 \text{ mol}}{261.35 \text{ g}} = 0.42 \text{ mol Ba(NO}_3)_2$$

Avogadro's Number

The number of particles in a mole is called **Avogadro's number**, or Avogadro's constant. This value is often rounded to 6.02×10^{23} units/mol. In other words, there are 6.02×10^{23} atoms of carbon in exactly 1 mole (mol) of carbon-12. There are 6.02×10^{23} molecules of sulfur dioxide in 1 mol of SO_2 gas. The amount in moles can be converted to the number of particles, as shown in the following example.

$$2.5 \text{ mol CO}_2 \times \frac{6.02 \times 10^{23} \text{ molecules}}{1 \text{ mol CO}_2} = 1.5 \times 10^{24} \text{ molecules CO}_2$$

Similarly, the number of particles can be converted to the amount in moles, as shown in the following example.

$$3.01 \times 10^{23} \text{ molecules CO}_2 \times \frac{1 \text{ mol CO}_2}{6.02 \times 10^{23} \text{ molecules}} = 0.500 \text{ mol CO}_2$$

Percentage Composition and Chemical Formulas

Chemists sometimes have to determine the formula of a compound, especially one that they may have just synthesized. A chemical formula is determined by calculating the **percentage composition** of the compound. The percentage composition represents the percentage by mass of each element in the compound. The molar mass of each element is then used to determine the simplest ratio of the elements to arrive at the formula. A formula that shows the simplest ratio of elements is called an **empirical formula**. For example, suppose that chemical analysis of a dead alkaline battery shows that it contains a compound that consists of 69.6% Mn and 30.4% O.

First, assume that you have a 100.0 g sample of the compound. Therefore, you would have 69.6 g Mn and 30.4 g O. Next, convert these masses to amounts in moles.

$$69.6 \text{ g Mn} \times \frac{1 \text{ mol Mn}}{54.94 \text{ g}} = 1.27 \text{ mol Mn}$$

$$30.4 \text{ g O} \times \frac{1 \text{ mol O}}{16 \text{ g}} = 1.9 \text{ mol O}$$

Therefore, the simplest ratio is 1.27 mol Mn: 1.9 mol O. Chemical formulas are always written in simplest whole numbers. As a result, the empirical formula for this compound is written as Mn_2O_3.

A compound can also be represented by a **molecular formula**, which is a whole-number multiple of its empirical formula. The molar mass of the compound is used to determine the molecular formula from its empirical formula. For example, suppose a compound has the empirical formula NH_2. The molar mass of this compound is determined to be 32.06 g/mol. The following equation can be used to determine the molecular formula.

n(molar mass of empirical formula) = molar mass of compound where n is a whole number

In the case of NH_2, $n(16.03 \text{ g/mol}) = (32.06 \text{ g/mol})$ or $n = 2$. The molecular formula is determined by multiplying the empirical formula by 2 to get N_2H_4.

Just as you can calculate a chemical formula from percentage composition, you can also calculate the percentage composition from a chemical formula. Once again, you must use the molar mass. For example, suppose you want to determine the percentage composition of Fe_3C, a compound in cast iron. The molar mass of this compound is 179.56 g/mol. The subscripts indicate a ratio of 3Fe:1C. Therefore, the percentage composition is calculated as follows.

$$\text{mass \% Fe} = \frac{167.55 \text{ g Fe}}{179.56 \text{ g}} \times 100 = 93.31\% \text{ Fe}$$

$$\text{mass \% C} = \frac{12.01 \text{ g}}{179.56 \text{ g}} \times 100 = 6.69\% \text{ C}$$

Molarity

Substances are often dissolved in water to make a solution. The substance that is dissolved is called a **solute**. The substance in which the solute is dissolved is called a **solvent**. Water is often referred to as a universal solvent because it dissolves so many substances. The amount of solute that is dissolved in a solvent determines the concentration of the solution. The concentration of a solution is usually expressed in terms of its **molarity**. The molarity of a solution is defined as the moles of solute dissolved per liter of solution. For example, 1 mol of HCl dissolved in water to make 1 L of solution is a 1 molar (M) solution.

The formula for molarity is written as follows.

$$\text{molarity} = \frac{\text{moles of solute}}{\text{liters of solution}}$$

Suppose 400 mL of a solution contains 85 g KCl. To calculate the molarity of this solution, first determine the number of moles of KCl present.

$$85 \text{ g} \times \frac{1 \text{ mol}}{74.55 \text{ g}} = 1.14 \text{ mol KCl}$$

Next, calculate the volume of this solution in liters.

$$400 \text{ mL} \times \frac{1 \text{ L}}{1000 \text{ mL}} = 0.400 \text{ L}$$

Finally, use the formula to calculate the molarity of this solution.

$$\text{molarity} = \frac{1.14 \text{ moles}}{0.400 \text{ L}} = 2.85 \text{ moles/L} = 2.85M$$

Mole Ratios

The coefficients in a chemical equation represent mole ratios. Consider the equation: $N_2 + 3H_2 \rightarrow 2NH_3$, which shows the synthesis of ammonia gas from nitrogen and hydrogen gases. This equation states that 1 mol N_2 reacts with 3 mol H_2 to produce 2 mol NH_3. You can use these mole ratios to make certain calculations. For example, this equation allows you to calculate how many moles of N_2 are needed to react with 312 mol H_2.

$$? \text{ mol } N_2 = 312 \text{ mol } H_2 \times \frac{1 \text{ mol } N_2}{3 \text{ mol } H_2} = 104 \text{ mol } N_2$$

You learned that the molar mass of a substance allows you to convert between moles and mass. Therefore, you can also calculate how many grams of N_2 are required.

$$? \text{ g } N_2 = 104 \text{ mol } N_2 \times \frac{28.02 \text{ g } N_2}{\text{mol } N_2} = 2914 \text{ g } N_2$$

The above equation for the synthesis of ammonia can also be read in terms of volume because all the reactants and products are gases. Therefore, the equation can be read as 1 L N_2 reacts with 3 L H_2 to produce 2 L NH_3.

Consider the following equation which shows the decomposition of water by electricity to produce hydrogen and oxygen gases.

$$2H_2O + \text{electricity} \rightarrow 2H_2 + O_2$$

This equation states that the volume of hydrogen gas produced will be twice the volume of oxygen gas produced. Experiments confirm what this equation predicts.

Moles and Gas Laws

Moles are also used in certain problems involving gas laws. For example, the **ideal gas law** relates all four gas variables, including pressure, temperature, volume, and the number of moles of a gas. When any three of these variables are given, the fourth can be calculated with the use of the following equation.

$$PV = nRT$$

R is a proportionality constant and equals 8.314 $(L \bullet kPa)(mol \bullet K)$, if the pressure is given in kPa units, and R equals 0.0821$(L \bullet atm)(mol \bullet K)$, if the pressure unit is expressed in atmospheres.

Molar mass is needed to solve problems involving Graham's law of effusion. **Effusion** is the passage of a gas under pressure through a tiny opening. This law states that the rate of effusion of a gas is inversely proportional to the square root of the gas's molar mass. The following equation is used to solve problems involving Graham's law of effusion.

$$\frac{v_A}{v_B} = \sqrt{\frac{M_B}{M_A}}$$

In the above equation, v_A and v_B represent the molecular speeds of gases A and B, while M_A and M_B represent their molar masses. Notice that the relationship between molecular speed and molar mass is an inverse one.

UNIT 5

Review

Darken the circle by the best answer.

1. The unit for molar mass is

   Ⓐ grams per atoms.

   Ⓑ atoms per gram.

   Ⓒ mol/g.

   Ⓓ g/mol.

2. One mole of any element contains 6.02×10^{23}

   Ⓐ molecules.

   Ⓑ atoms.

   Ⓒ grams.

   Ⓓ g/mol.

3. If the empirical formula of a compound is known, then the

   Ⓐ molecular mass of the compound can be calculated.

   Ⓑ arrangement of the atoms is also known.

   Ⓒ percentage composition of each element can be determined.

   Ⓓ compound's actual formula is also known.

4. What is the concentration of a solution that contains 4.0 mol of a substance dissolved in 2.0 L of water?

   Ⓐ 1 M

   Ⓑ 2 M

   Ⓒ 4 M

   Ⓓ 8 M

5. The coefficients in all balanced chemical equations represent

   Ⓐ mole ratios.

   Ⓑ mass ratios.

   Ⓒ volume ratios.

   Ⓓ both the mole ratios and the mass ratios.

6. If 6 L N_2 is completely reacted with 6 L H_2 to produce NH_3, how many liters of *unreacted* gas remain?

   Ⓐ 12 L

   Ⓑ 6 L

   Ⓒ 4 L

   Ⓓ 1 L

7. How is a mole defined?

   _____

   _____

   _____

8. Why is a balanced chemical equation required to solve stoichiometry problems?

   _____

   _____

   _____

   _____

   _____

UNIT 5

Moles, Molar Mass, and Avogadro's Number

> The molar mass of a substance, either an element or a compound, is the mass in grams of one mole of a substance. The number of particles in a mole is called Avogadro's number, or Avogadro's constant. This value is often rounded to 6.02×10^{23} units/mol.

Determine the number of moles in each of the following substances.

1. 67.42 g Si _____

2. 11.82 g gold _____

3. 28.8 g Br_2 _____

4. 184.7 g sodium sulfate _____

5. 3.3 kg aluminum chromate _____

Determine the number of grams in each of the following substances.

6. 1 mol lead _____

7. 2.40 mol O_2 _____

8. 7.8 mol $ZnSO_4$ _____

9. 3.25 mol tin(II) chloride _____

10. 0.92 mol aluminum chromate _____

Determine the number of atoms or molecules in each of the following substances.

11. 0.30 mol F _____

12. 0.70 mol iron _____

13. 4.0 mol Na _____

14. 4.0 mol NH_3 _____

Determine the number of moles in each of the following substances.

15. 8.0×10^{13} atoms Ag _____

16. 5.7×10^{25} atoms potassium _____

17. 3.5×10^{23} molecules H_2O _____

18. 1.86×10^{25} molecules CH_4 _____

UNIT 5

Percentage Composition

The percentage composition represents the percentage by mass of each element in the compound.

Determine the percentage composition by mass of each of the following compounds.

1. SO_2

2. NH_4NO_3

3. $C_6H_{12}O_6$

4. $HC_2H_3O_2$

5. $Pb(CH_3COO)_2$

UNIT 5

Empirical Formulas

The percentage composition represents the percentage by mass of each element in the compound. The molar mass of each element is then used to determine the simplest ratio of the elements to arrive at the formula. A formula that shows the simplest ratio of elements is called an empirical formula.

Use the following percentage compositions to determine the empirical formula for each compound.

1. 63.52% Fe, 36.48% S

2. 74.51% Pb, 25.49% Cl

3. 26.58% K, 35.35% Cr, 38.07% O

4. 52.55% Ba, 10.72% N, 36.73% O

5. 29.15% N, 8.41% H, 12.50% C, 49.94% O

UNIT 5

Molecular Formulas

Use the following information to determine the molecular formula for each compound. The following equation can be used to determine the molecular formula.

n(molar mass of empirical formula) = molar mass of compound
where n is a whole number

1. empirical formula NO_2, molar mass 46 g/mol

2. empirical formula CH, molar mass 78 g/mol

3. empirical formula P_2O_5, molar mass 284 g/mol

4. empirical formula NH_2, molar mass 32.06 g/mol

5. empirical formula OCNCl, molar mass 232.41 g/mol

UNIT 5

Molarity

Use the formula for molarity to solve the following problems. The formula for molarity is written as follows.

$$\text{molarity} = \frac{\text{moles of solute}}{\text{liters of solution}}$$

1. Vinegar contains 5.0 g of acetic acid, CH_3COOH, in 100.0 mL of solution. What is the molarity of acetic acid in vinegar?

2. A solution is made by dissolving 29.66 g of $AgNO_3$ in 100.0 mL of water. What is the molarity of this solution?

3. If 20.0 g H_2SO_4 is dissolved to make 250.0 mL of a solution, what is the molarity of this solution?

4. How many grams of KBr must be dissolved to make 25.0 mL of a solution that has a molarity of 0.85 M?

5. If all the water in 430.0 mL of a 0.45 M NaCl solution evaporates, what mass of NaCl will remain?

UNIT 5

Mole-Mass Problems

Use the equation below to answer the following questions. The equation represents a reaction for gasoline combustion in a car's engine. A balanced equation indicates the mole ratios of reactants and products. The molar mass of a substance allows you to convert between moles and mass.

$$2C_8H_{18} + 25O_2 \rightarrow 16CO_2 + 18H_2O$$

1. How many moles of oxygen are required to react completely with 5 mol C_8H_{18}?

2. What mass of oxygen is required to completely react with 5 mol C_8H_{18}?

3. How many moles of CO_2 will be produced if the conditions in question 1 are met?

4. What is the mass of CO_2 produced if the conditions in question 1 are met?

5. What is the mass of H_2O produced if the conditions in question 1 are met?

UNIT 5 — Volume-Volume Problems

A car's catalytic converter combines carbon monoxide, a poisonous gas, with oxygen to form carbon dioxide gas. A balanced equation indicates the mole ratios of reactants and products. If all the reactants and products are gases, then the equation can also be read in terms of volume ratios.

1. Write the balanced equation for this reaction.

2. What volume of oxygen is required so that 630 mL of carbon monoxide gas is completely converted to carbon dioxide?

3. How many liters of carbon dioxide are produced if the catalytic converter processes 6.25 L of carbon monoxide?

4. How much oxygen does a catalytic converter require to produce 2.50 L of carbon dioxide?

5. Assume that 425 mL of carbon monoxide and 180 mL of oxygen are being processed by a catalytic converter. Will all of the carbon monoxide be converted to carbon dioxide? Explain your answer.

UNIT 5

Mass-Mass Problems

Dinitrogen oxide, commonly called laughing gas, is sometimes used as an anesthetic in dentistry. It is produced by the decomposition of ammonium nitrate. The other product of this reaction is water. A balanced equation indicates the mole ratios of reactants and products. The molar mass of a substance allows you to convert between moles and mass.

1. Write the balanced equation for the production of dinitrogen oxide and water from ammonium nitrate.

2. How many grams of ammonium nitrate are required to produce 66.0 g of dinitrogen oxide?

3. How many grams of water are produced by this reaction?

4. How many grams of laughing gas would be produced from the decomposition of 60 g of ammonium nitrate?

UNIT 5

Ideal Gas Law

The ideal gas law relates all four gas variables, including pressure, temperature, volume, and the number of moles of a gas. When any three of these variables are given, the fourth can be calculated with the use of the following equation.

$$PV = nRT$$

R is a proportionality constant and equals 8.314 (L•kPa)(mol•K), if the pressure is given in kPa units, and R equals 0.0821(L•atm)(mol•K), if the pressure unit is expressed in atmospheres.

Use the ideal gas law to answer the questions.

1. What is the pressure in atmospheres exerted by a 0.500 mol sample of oxygen gas in a 10.0 L container at 298K?

2. What is the volume, in liters, of 0.250 mol of hydrogen gas at 20°C and 0.974 atm pressure?

3. A sample of neon gas occupies 8.77 L at 20°C. What is the pressure, in atmospheres, exerted by 1.45 mol of this gas?

4. A sample of CO_2 gas with a mass of 0.30 g is placed in a 250 mL container at 400 K. What is the pressure in atmospheres exerted by this gas? Hint: Be sure to change mass to moles.

UNIT 5

Graham's Law of Effusion

This law states that the rate of effusion of a gas is inversely proportional to the square root of the gas's molar mass. The following equation is used to solve problems involving Graham's law of effusion.

$$\frac{v_A}{v_B} = \sqrt{\frac{M_B}{M_A}}$$

In the above equation, v_A and v_B represent the molecular speeds of gases A and B, while M_A and M_B represent their molar masses.

Use Graham's Law of Effusion to answer the questions.

1. At the same temperature, which gas travels faster, O_2 or N_2? Explain your answer.

_____

_____

_____

2. How much faster does H_2 gas travel compared to O_2 gas under the same conditions?

_____

_____

3. The average velocity of ammonia, NH_3, molecules at room temperature is 658 m/s. How fast would hydrogen sulfide, H_2S, molecules travel on average under the same conditions?

4. The average velocity of CO_2 molecules at room temperature is 409 m/s. What is the molar mass of a gas whose molecules have an average velocity of 322 m/s under the same conditions?

5. A sample of helium, He, effuses through the tiny pores in a balloon 6.50 times faster than does unknown gas X. What is the molar mass of the unknown gas?

Vinegar and grapefruit juice have a tart, sour taste. The substances in vinegar and grapefruit juice that give them this taste are known as acids. Soap and ammonia have a slippery feeling. The substances in soap and ammonia that make them feel slippery are known as bases. Acids and bases make up an important group of chemical compounds, found not only in homes, but everywhere.

Properties of Acids

Acids share certain physical and chemical properties. For example, acids react with many metals to produce hydrogen gas. An example is hydrochloric acid, HCl, which reacts with zinc metal, as shown by the following equation.

$$2HCl + Zn \rightarrow ZnCl_2 + H_2$$

Acids also produce solutions that conduct electricity well. Acid solutions are excellent conductors because acids dissociate in water to produce ions. An example is seen when HCl is added to water, as shown by the following equation.

$$HCl + H_2O \rightarrow H_3O^+ + Cl^-$$

HCl dissociates to produce a hydrogen ion, H^+, which immediately reacts with water to produce a hydronium ion, H_3O^+. A hydronium ion is an **electrolyte**, which is a substance that conducts electricity when present in a solution.

Another property shared by acids is their ability to generate hydronium ions. Those acids that dissociate completely to form many hydronium ions are known as strong acids. Hydrochloric acid, HCl, is a strong acid. In contrast, hypochlorous acid, HOCl, is a weak acid because it dissociates only partially. As a result, relatively few hydronium ions are produced.

Because of this last property, a Swedish chemist named Svante Arrhenius proposed in 1890 that an acid was defined as any substance that, when added to water, increases the

Key Terms

electrolyte—a substance that conducts electricity when present in a solution

Brønsted-Lowry acid—a substance that donates a proton to another substance

Brønsted-Lowry base—a substance that accepts a proton from another substance

conjugate acid—an acid that forms when a base gains a proton

conjugate base—a base that forms when an acid loses a proton

pH—a value used to express acidity or alkalinity of a solution; it is defined as the logarithm of the reciprocal of the concentration of hydronium ions

normality—the molarity of the solution times the number of either H_3O^+ ions or OH^- ions produced per molecule of substance

titration—a method to determine the concentration of a substance in solution by adding a solution of known volume and concentration until the reaction is completed

hydronium ion concentration. However, problems arose with the Arrhenius definition. For example, this definition applies only to solutions. However, HCl can also exist as a gas.

In 1923, two scientists proposed a different definition of an acid. They defined an acid as a substance that donates a proton, H^+, to another substance. This became known as the Brønsted-Lowry definition. A **Brønsted-Lowry acid** is defined as a proton donor. The following equations show how HCl donates a proton to H_2O. First, HCl dissociates.

$$HCl \rightarrow H^+ + Cl^-$$

Then, the proton reacts with a water molecule.

$$H^+ + H_2O \rightarrow H_3O^+$$

Properties of Bases

Like acids, bases produce electrolytes when dissolved in solution. Bases can be either strong or weak, depending on how much they dissociate. Bases generate hydroxide ion, OH^-, in solution. This property is the basis of the Arrhenius definition of a base. He defined a base as any substance that, when added to water, increases the hydroxide ion concentration. For example, NaOH is an example of an Arrhenius acid, as shown by the following equation.

$$NaOH \rightarrow Na^+ + OH^-$$

As you might expect, this definition was changed. A **Brønsted-Lowry base** is a substance that accepts a proton. For example, in the following equation, ammonia, NH_3, is a base because it accepts a proton from H_2O.

$$NH_3 + H_2O \rightarrow NH_4^+ + OH^-$$

Notice that in the above reaction, H_2O acts as an acid because it donates a proton.

Conjugate Acids and Bases

Look again at the reaction between ammonia, a base, and water, which acts as an acid.

$$NH_3 + H_2O \rightarrow NH_4^+ + OH^-$$

Notice that NH_3 acts as a base by accepting a proton and forming NH_4^+. The ammonium ion, NH_4^+, is known as the **conjugate acid** of the base ammonia, NH_3. Notice also that H_2O acts as an acid by donating a proton and forming OH^-. The hydroxide ion, OH^-, is known as the **conjugate base** of the acid, water. Every Brønsted-Lowry acid has a conjugate base, and every Brønsted-Lowry base has a conjugate acid.

pH

Examine the following equation.

$$H_2O + H_2O \rightarrow H_3O^+ + OH^-$$

Notice that water is both an acid and a base. Both hydronium and hydroxide ions are formed in equal amounts. Experiments show that the concentration of these ions is 1.00×10^{-7} M at 25°C.

$$[H_3O^+] = [OH^-] = 1 \times 10^{-7} \text{ M}$$

In 1909, a Danish chemist named Søren Sørensen, proposed that the acidity or basicity of a solution be described in terms of the negative of the power of 10, or the negative logarithm of $[H_3O^+]$. He called this measure **pH**. The letters p and H represent powers of hydrogen. In the case of pure water, $[H_3O^+] = [OH^-] = 1 \times 10^{-7}$ M. Therefore, the pH of this solution is 7. We say that the solution is neutral. In contrast, a solution where the $[H_3O^+] = 1 \times 10^{-4}$, the pH is 4.

If you know the $[H_3O^+]$, you can calculate the $[OH^-]$ because $[H_3O^+][OH^-] = 1.00 \times 10^{-14}$. Therefore, if the $[H_3O^+] = 1 \times 10^{-4}$ M, then the $[OH^-] = 1 \times 10^{-10}$ M.

Normality

In addition to molarity, concentration can also be expressed in terms of **normality**. The normality of a solution can be defined as the molarity of the solution times the number of either H_3O^+ ions or OH^- ions produced per molecule of substance. For example, consider a 1 M HCl solution. One molecule of HCl dissociates in solution to form 1 H_3O^+ ion and 1 Cl^- ion. Therefore, the normality of a 1 M HCl solution is $1 \times 1 = 1$ N.

Next, consider a 1 M H_2SO_4 solution. In this case, one molecule of H_2SO_4 dissociates in solution to form 2 H_3O^+ ions and 1 SO_4^{2-} ion. Therefore, the normality of a 1 M H_2SO_4 solution is $1 \times 2 = 2$ N. For the same reason, the normality of a 2 M $Ba(OH)_2$ solution is $2 \times 2 = 4$ N.

Titration

Acids and bases are often used to perform a **titration**. To perform a titration, a solution of known volume and concentration is added to a known volume of a solution whose concentration is unknown. Simply stated, the purpose of a titration is to determine the concentration of an acid or a base.

A common use of a titration is to check the levels of certain chemicals in swimming pools. For example, a titration is done to check the pH, or hydronium ion concentration, of pool water. The end point is reached when a certain color change is observed. Ideally, the titration should indicate that the pH of the pool water falls between 7.2 and 7.6.

The following equation is used when performing calculations involving titrations.

[concentration of acid][volume of acid] = [concentration of base][volume of base]

For example, assume that 40.00 mL of HCl of unknown concentration are needed to neutralize 24.64 mL of a 0.5500 M NaOH solution. The equation above is used to calculate the concentration of the acid solution.

[? M HCl][40.00 mL HCl] = [0.5500 M NaOH][24.64 mL NaOH]

$$? \text{ M HCl} = \frac{[0.5500 \text{ M NaOH}][24.64 \text{ mL NaOH}]}{[40.00 \text{ mL HCl}]} =$$

0.338 M HCl

The concentrations can be expressed in either molarity or normality. However, the units for both concentration and volume must be the same on both sides of the equation.

UNIT 6

Review

Darken the circle by the best answer.

1. The stronger an acid is, the
   - Ⓐ more hydroxide ions produced in solution.
   - Ⓑ more hydronium ions produced in solution.
   - Ⓒ stronger its conjugate base.
   - Ⓓ weaker its conjugate acid.

2. A solution containing an Arrhenius base would have
   - Ⓐ a pH less than 7.
   - Ⓑ a pH of 7.
   - Ⓒ a pH greater than 7.
   - Ⓓ no measurable pH.

3. According to the Brønsted-Lowry definition, a proton acceptor is a(n)
   - Ⓐ acid.
   - Ⓑ base.
   - Ⓒ electrolyte.
   - Ⓓ hydronium ion.

4. Which of the following is the conjugate base of the acid HCl?
   - Ⓐ H^+
   - Ⓑ OH^-
   - Ⓒ H_3O^+
   - Ⓓ Cl^-

5. Which solution would have a pH value greater than 7?
   - Ⓐ $[OH^-] = 2.5 \times 10^{-2}$ M
   - Ⓑ $[OH^-] = 4.4 \times 10^{-9}$ M
   - Ⓒ $[OH^-] = 1.0 \times 10^{-7}$ M
   - Ⓓ 0.001 M HCl

6. Which solution has the greatest normality?
   - Ⓐ 0.1 M HCl
   - Ⓑ 1 M NaOH
   - Ⓒ 3 M HF
   - Ⓓ 2 M $Mg(OH)_2$

7. The two variables involved in a titration are
   - Ⓐ molarity and normality.
   - Ⓑ concentration and volume.
   - Ⓒ hydronium and hydroxide ion concentrations.
   - Ⓓ volumes of the acid and base used in the titration.

8. Explain why ammonia, NH_3, is not considered an Arrhenius base but is considered a Brønsted-Lowry base.

   _____

   _____

9. Calculate the molarity of an acid if 25.5 mL of this acid is used to titrate 42.3 mL of 1.25 M NaOH.

UNIT 6 Brønsted-Lowry Acids and Bases

> *According to the Brønsted-Lowry definitions, an acid is a proton donor, while a base is a proton acceptor.*

Label the acid and base in each of the following equations, based on the Brønsted-Lowry definitions.

1. $H_2SO_4 + H_2O \rightarrow H_3O^+ + HSO_4^-$

2. $CO_3^{2-} + H_2O \rightarrow HCO_3^- + OH^-$

3. $NH_4^+ + OH^- \rightarrow NH_3 + H_2O$

4. $HCOOH + CH_3COO^- \rightarrow HCOO^- + CH_3COOH$

5. $H_2O + CH_3COOH \rightarrow CH_3COO^- + H_3O^+$

6. $HCN + H_2O \rightarrow CN^- + H_3O^+$

7. $C_6H_5NH_2 + H_2O \rightarrow C_6H_5NH_3^+ + OH^-$

8. $H_2O + H_2O \rightarrow H_3O^+ + OH^-$

UNIT 6

Conjugate Acids and Bases

Identify the conjugate acid-base pairs in the following reactions. An acid donates a proton to become a conjugate base. A base accepts a proton to form a conjugate acid.

1. $HCO_3^- + NH_3 \rightarrow CO_3^{2-} + NH_4^+$

_____

2. $HCl + H_2O \rightarrow H_3O^+ + Cl^-$

_____

3. $CH_3COOH + H_2O \rightarrow H_3O^+ + CH_3COO^-$

_____

4. $HOCl + NH_3 \rightarrow NH_4^+ + ClO^-$

_____

5. $H_2SO_4 + OH^- \rightarrow HSO_4^- + H_2O$

_____

Write the formulas for the conjugate bases formed by each of the following acids.

6. $H_2PO_4^-$ _____   7. HCN _____

8. H_2O _____   9. HOOCCOOH _____

Write the formulas for the conjugate acids formed by each of the following bases.

10. F^- _____   11. OH^- _____

12. H_2O _____   13. NH_3 _____

UNIT 6

pH

The pH value equals the negative logarithm of the hydronium ion, H_3O^+, concentration. A pH value greater than 7 is basic, while a pH value less than 7 is acidic. The product of the H_3O^+ and OH^- concentrations equals 1×10^{-14}.

Complete the following table.

Sample	pH	$[H_3O^+]$	$[OH^-]$	Acidic or Basic
rain water	5	_____	_____	_____
window-cleaning liquid	_____	1×10^{-11} M	_____	_____
stomach contents	_____	_____	1×10^{-12} M	_____
black coffee	_____	1×10^{-5} M	_____	_____
hand soap	10	_____	_____	_____
apple juice	_____	_____	1×10^{-11} M	_____
drain cleaner	_____	1×10^{-13} M	_____	_____
baking soda	9	_____	_____	_____
antacid	_____	_____	1×10^{-6} M	_____
pure water	_____	_____	1×10^{-7} M	_____

Unit 6, Acids and Bases
Chemistry, SV 0424-7

UNIT 6

Molarity and Normality

The normality of a solution can be defined as the molarity of the solution times the number of either H_3O^+ ions or OH^- ions produced per molecule of substance.

Solve the following problems.

1. What is the normality of a 0.6 M KOH solution?

2. What is the normality of a 1.2 M $Ca(OH)_2$ solution?

3. A solution of H_3PO_4 is 6 N. What is the molarity of this solution?

4. How many grams of NaOH must be used to make 1 L of a 0.80 N NaOH solution?

5. A one-liter solution is made by dissolving 96.4 g of $Mg(OH)_2$ in water. Calculate both the molarity and normality of this solution.

6. How many grams of $Ca(OH)_2$ must be dissolved to make 550 mL of a 1.2 N solution?

UNIT 6

Titration

Solve the following problems. The following equation is used when performing calculations involving titrations.

[concentration of acid][volume of acid] = [concentration of base][volume of base]

1. If 20.0 mL of 0.01 M HCl solution is required to neutralize 30.0 mL of NaOH solution, what is the molarity of the base?

2. Suppose that 20.0 mL of a 0.10 M $Ca(OH)_2$ solution is required to neutralize 12.0 mL of HCl solution, what is the molarity of the HCl solution?

3. What volume of 2.5×10^{-2} M H_2SO_4 is required to neutralize 125 mL of 0.03 M KOH?

4. What volume of 2.5×10^{-2} M H_2SO_4 is required to neutralize 125 mL of 0.03 M $Mg(OH)_2$?

5. It required 11 mL of 0.01 M KOH to neutralize a 5.00 L sample of acid rain. Calculate the concentration of hydronium ions in the rain sample.

UNIT 6

Acid-Base Word Search

Locate the following words in the puzzle below.

1. ion that forms in an acidic solution _____

2. proton acceptor _____

3. process of adding NaOH of known volume and concentration to a known volume of HCl to determine its concentration _____

4. what CN^- forms after reacting with an acid _____

5. pH of solution with 1×10^{-7} M H_3O^+ _____

6. proton donor _____

7. pH of a solution with 1×10^{-3} M OH^- _____

```
E  C  R  H  H  U  C  Y  D  O  U  O  D  W  N
K  Z  Y  Z  R  R  W  V  Q  C  F  U  X  R  H
O  E  H  N  E  K  K  L  V  B  B  W  C  N  S
L  M  X  X  C  O  S  H  G  I  P  N  C  T  D
J  F  U  S  T  L  M  D  X  K  O  E  B  L  M
S  R  Z  I  V  Y  V  I  Y  I  L  U  Q  J  J
I  V  Z  P  N  X  B  C  T  E  U  T  Z  L  K
A  N  M  I  Z  O  O  A  V  D  Z  R  G  Y  Q
B  W  F  J  B  V  R  E  S  T  R  A  U  L  D
U  J  B  P  K  T  N  D  T  E  M  L  X  N  G
C  C  V  G  I  L  X  B  Y  N  H  K  N  I  Q
B  G  B  T  J  E  Y  N  C  H  J  Q  X  B  E
S  S  A  L  W  A  L  C  F  W  H  A  S  U  F
```

Most compounds that contain the element carbon are classified as **organic compounds**. In addition to carbon, organic compounds also contain hydrogen, and usually oxygen. Nitrogen, phosphorus, and sulfur are sometimes also present. More than 12 million organic compounds are known. To make it easier to study them, organic compounds with similar properties are placed in a group. The group that contains the simplest organic compounds contains the hydrocarbons.

Hydrocarbons

A **hydrocarbon** contains only carbon and hydrogen. Hydrocarbons are subdivided into three smaller groups, depending on the type of bonding between the carbon atoms. The simplest hydrocarbons are the **alkanes**, which consist of carbon atoms that are connected only by single bonds. The general formula for an alkane is C_nH_{2n+2}, where n represents the number of carbon atoms. The structural formulas for three alkanes are shown below.

methane, CH_4 ethane, C_2H_6 propane, C_3H_8

Key Terms

organic compound—with some exceptions, any compound that contains the element carbon

hydrocarbon—an organic compound composed only of hydrogen and carbon

alkanes—the simplest hydrocarbons which consist of carbon atoms that are connected only by single bonds

alkenes—hydrocarbons which consist of at least one double bond between two carbon atoms

alkynes—hydrocarbons which consist of at least one triple bond between two carbon atoms

functional group—the portion of a molecule that is active in a chemical reaction and that determines the properties of many organic compounds

isomer—one of two or more compounds that have the same chemical composition but different structures

substitution reaction—a type of chemical reaction where one or more atoms replace another atom or group of atoms in a molecule

addition reaction—a type of chemical reaction where an atom or molecule is added to an unsaturated molecule

polymer—a large molecule that is formed by joining five or more smaller units called monomers

condensation reaction—a reaction where two molecules combine, usually with the loss of a water molecule

hydrolysis reaction—a reaction where a water molecule is added and the bond between two monomers is broken

elimination reaction—a reaction where a simple molecule, such as water or ammonia, is removed from a compound to produce a new substance

Alkenes contain at least one double bond between two carbon atoms. The general formula for an alkene is C_nH_{2n}. The structural formulas for two alkenes are shown below.

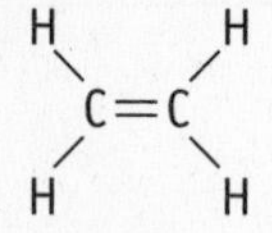

ethene 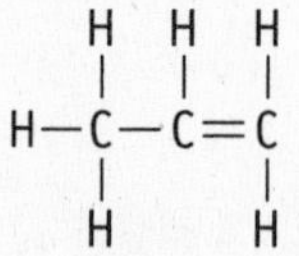   **propene**

Alkynes contain at least one triple bond between two two carbon atoms. The general formula for an alkyne is C_nH_{2n-2}. The simplest alkyne is ethyne: $H-C\equiv C-H$.

Functional Groups

Many organic compounds contain a **functional group**, which is a group of atoms that determines the properties of the molecule. Organic compounds are commonly classified by the functional group they contain. For example, the functional group —OH on one of the C atoms classifies the molecule as an alcohol. Other classes of organic compounds have different functional groups.

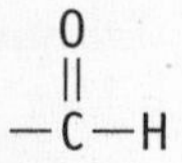

aldehyde 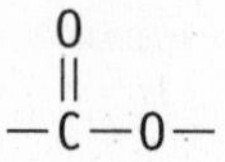   **ester** 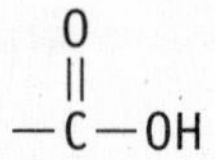   **carboxylic acid**

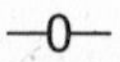

ether 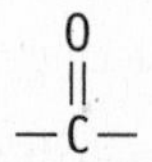   **ketone**

Isomers

Two different organic compounds can have the same molecular formula. For example, two different alcohols have the molecular formula $C_4H_{10}O$. However, the way these atoms are arranged differs in each molecule. These two molecules are known as **isomers**, which are molecules that have the same chemical composition but different structures. As a result of their different structures, isomers have different physical and chemical properties.

Naming Hydrocarbons

Organic compounds have their own naming system, which includes prefixes, suffixes, and numbers. For example, C_3H_8 is called propane. The prefix *pro-* indicates that the compound has three C atoms. The suffix *–ane* indicates that it is an alkane. An alkene with three C atoms is called propene, while an alkyne with three C atoms is called propyne.

Alkenes and alkynes with four or more C atoms must also include one or more numbers to show the position of the multiple bonds. Only the C atoms are numbered. The first carbon atom with a multiple bond must have the lowest number. Examine the following structural formulas.

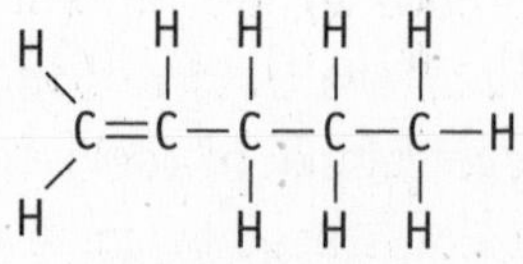

1-pentene

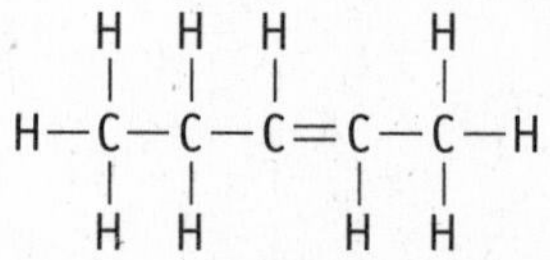

2-pentene

The name *1-pentene* indicates that the double bond is present between the first and second carbon atoms. The name *2-pentene* indicates that the double bond is present between the second and third carbon atoms.

If there is more than one multiple bond, then the position of each multiple bond must be indicated. For example, examine the following structural formula.

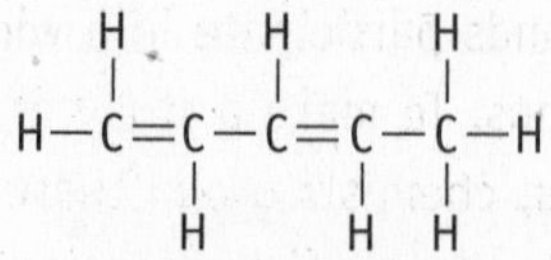

1,3-pentadiene

The above alkene is named 1,3-pentadiene. The numbers 1 and 3 indicate the position of the double bonds, while the prefix *di-* indicates that two double bonds are present.

You must be careful when numbering the carbon atoms in a hydrocarbon that is not a simple straight chain. Examine the following structural formula.

$$H-\underset{\underset{H}{|}}{\overset{\overset{H}{|}}{C}}-\underset{\underset{H-\underset{\underset{H-\underset{\underset{H}{|}}{\overset{\overset{H}{|}}{C_1}}-H}{|}}{\overset{\overset{H}{|}}{C_2}}-H}{|}}{\overset{\overset{H}{|}}{C_3}}-\underset{\underset{H}{|}}{\overset{\overset{H}{|}}{C_4}}-\underset{\underset{H}{|}}{\overset{\overset{H}{|}}{C_5}}-\underset{\underset{H}{|}}{\overset{\overset{H}{|}}{C_6}}-\underset{\underset{H}{|}}{\overset{\overset{H}{|}}{C_7}}-H$$

Notice that numbers are assigned to the carbon atoms that make up the longest chain. The longest or "parent" chain in the above compound contains seven C atoms. As a result, the "parent" compound is heptane. Notice also that the numbering is done so that any branches on the chain have the lowest possible numbers. In the above compound, a methyl group, $-CH_3$, is present on the third carbon. Therefore, the name for the above compound is 3, methyl-heptane.

The same system is used to name organic compounds that contain functional groups. For example, examine the following structural formula.

$$H-\underset{\underset{H}{|}}{\overset{\overset{H}{|}}{C}}-\underset{\underset{O}{|}}{\overset{\overset{H}{|}}{C}}-\underset{\underset{H}{|}}{\overset{\overset{H}{|}}{C}}-H$$
$$\underset{H}{|}$$

The compound above is named 2-propanol. The prefix *prop-* indicates that there are three C atoms present. The suffix *–ol* indicates that this compound is an alcohol, while the number 2 indicates the position of the $-OH$ functional group.

Organic Reactions

Organic compounds participate in a wide variety of chemical reactions. To make a study of these reactions somewhat easier, chemists group these reactions in several types. One type of reaction is called a **substitution reaction** where one or more atoms replace another atom or group of atoms in a molecule. An example of a substitution reaction is shown by the following equation.

$$CH_4 + Cl_2 \rightarrow CH_3Cl + HCl$$

In this substitution reaction, a Cl atom replaces a H atom on the methane molecule. This substitution is easier to see if the structural formulas are shown.

$$H-\underset{\underset{H}{|}}{\overset{\overset{H}{|}}{C}}-H + Cl-Cl \longrightarrow H-\underset{\underset{H}{|}}{\overset{\overset{H}{|}}{C}}-Cl + H-Cl$$

methane   chlorine   chloromethane   hydrogen chloride

Another type of chemical reaction involving organic compounds is called an **addition reaction**. In an addition reaction, an atom or molecule is added to an unsaturated molecule. A common addition reaction is hydrogenation, which is the process in which vegetable oil is changed into a solid fat. The following equation illustrates hydrogenation. The brackets indicate that only a portion of the very long oil and fat molecules are shown.

$$\left(-\underset{\underset{H}{|}}{\overset{\overset{H}{|}}{C}}-\underset{}{\overset{\overset{H}{|}}{C}}=\underset{}{\overset{\overset{H}{|}}{C}}-\underset{\underset{H}{|}}{\overset{\overset{H}{|}}{C}}-\underset{}{\overset{\overset{H}{|}}{C}}=\underset{}{\overset{\overset{H}{|}}{C}}-\underset{\underset{H}{|}}{\overset{\overset{H}{|}}{C}}-\right) + H_2 \xrightarrow{\text{catalyst}}$$

oil

$$\left(-\underset{\underset{H}{|}}{\overset{\overset{H}{|}}{C}}-\underset{}{\overset{\overset{H}{|}}{C}}=\underset{\underset{H}{|}}{\overset{\overset{H}{|}}{C}}-\underset{\underset{H}{|}}{\overset{\overset{H}{|}}{C}}-\underset{\underset{H}{|}}{\overset{\overset{H}{|}}{C}}-\underset{\underset{H}{|}}{\overset{\overset{H}{|}}{C}}-\underset{\underset{H}{|}}{\overset{\overset{H}{|}}{C}}-\right)$$

fat

Addition reactions are used to form **polymers**. A polymer is a large molecule that is formed by joining five or more smaller units called monomers. One polymer made by an addition reaction is polyethylene, a strong but flexible plastic used to make a variety of consumer products including bottles. Polyethylene is made from C_2H_4, ethene which serves as the monomer. The following shows how two ethene molecules are added to form a larger molecule. The open bonds at both ends indicate that more ethene molecules can be added to form the polymer.

$$CH_2{=}CH_2 + CH_2{=}CH_2 \longrightarrow -CH_2-CH_2-CH_2-CH_2-$$

Polymers can also be formed by a **condensation reaction**. In a condensation reaction, two molecules combine, usually with the loss of a water molecule. Condensation reactions are used to form a variety of consumer products such as nylon and a compound called PET, which is used to make permanent-press clothing.

Condensation reactions are also involved in the synthesis of carbohydrates, lipids, and proteins. For example, the following equation shows how two amino acids are combined with the loss of a water molecule.

The link that joins the N and C atoms of two different amino acids is called a peptide bond. Hundreds of peptide bonds are formed by condensation reactions to synthesize a protein.

Polymers, including carbohydrates, lipids, and proteins, are decomposed to form monomers during a **hydrolysis reaction**. In a hydrolysis reaction, a water molecule is added, and the bond between two monomers is broken. Hydrolysis is the reverse of the condensation reaction. Therefore, an example of a hydrolysis reaction would be the previous equation, this time going from right to left.

Still another type of reaction involving organic compounds is an **elimination reaction**. In an elimination reaction, a simple molecule, such as water or ammonia, is removed from a compound to produce a new substance. Some elimination reactions are similar to condensation reactions in that they both produce a water molecule. The following is an example of an elimination reaction that produces water as a byproduct.

ethanol   **ethane**   **water**

Notice that H and OH are removed from ethanol to produce ethene. The H and OH combine to form water.

UNIT 7

Review

Darken the circle by the best answer.

1. Which formula represents an alkene?

   (A) C_2H_2

   (B) C_4H_8

   (C) C_6H_6

   (D) C_6H_{10}

2. Which compound can be a carboxylic acid?

   (A) C_2H_4OH

   (B) $C_5H_{10}O$

   (C) C_6H_{12}

   (D) $C_4H_8O_2$

3. Which compound can have the greatest number of isomers?

   (A) C_2H_6

   (B) C_3H_8

   (C) C_6H_6

   (D) $C_{20}H_{42}$

4. When naming a hydrocarbon,

   (A) the number of carbon atoms in the molecule is not important.

   (B) the names of any side chains can be omitted.

   (C) begin by identifying and numbering the longest carbon chain.

   (D) include the positions of all single bonds.

5. What happens as a result of a condensation reaction?

   (A) A water molecule is formed.

   (B) Single bonds replace all double bonds in the reactants.

   (C) An alcohol is converted to an alkane.

   (D) Monomers are formed.

6. Which molecule cannot be a reactant in an addition reaction?

   (A) C_2H_4

   (B) C_2H_6

   (C) C_6H_6

   (D) $C_{10}H_{18}$

7. What product is formed when fluorine reacts with methane in a substitution reaction?

   (A) F_2

   (B) H_2O

   (C) CH_4

   (D) CH_3F

8. Explain why ethane does not react like ethene when it is mixed with Cl_2 under the same conditions.

   _____

   _____

   _____

   _____

   _____

UNIT 7

Hydrocarbons

- A **hydrocarbon** is an organic compound composed only of hydrogen and carbon.
- An **alkane** has carbon atoms connected by single bonds. The structural formula for an alkane is C_nH_{2n+2}.
- An **alkene** contains one or more double bonds. The structural formula for an alkene is C_nH_{2n}.
- An **alkyne** contains one or more triple bonds. The general formula for an alkyne is C_nH_{2n-2}.

Draw the structural formula for each of the following compounds.
Label each compound as either an *alkane*, *alkene*, or *alkyne*.

1. C_4H_{10}

2. C_4H_8

3. C_3H_4

4. C_5H_{10}

5. Draw the structural formula for an alkyne with five carbon atoms.

UNIT 7

Functional Groups

> *A functional group is the portion of a molecule that is active in a chemical reaction and that determines the properties of many organic compounds.*

Classify each of the following organic compounds as an alcohol, aldehyde, carboxylic acid, ester, ether, or ketone. Then draw its structural formula. Begin by identifying the functional group.

1. $CH_3CH_2CH_2COOH$

_____

2. $CH_3CH_2CH_2COCH_3$

_____

3. $HOCH_2CHOHCH_2OH$

_____

4. $CH_3CH_2OCH_2CH_3$

_____

5. $CH_3CH_2CH_2COOCH_2CH_3$

_____

UNIT 7

Isomers

> **Isomers have the same molecular formulas but different structural formulas.**

1. Draw the structural formulas for two isomers of C_4H_{10}.

2. Can two compounds with the molecular formulas C_4H_{10} and $C_4H_{10}O$ be isomers of one another? Explain your answer.

_____

_____

3. Explain why isomers have different chemical and physical properties.

_____

_____

4. Draw two structural formulas for an alcohol with the molecular formula C_3H_8O.

5. Draw an isomer for the following organic compound.

```
    H  O  H  O  H
    |  ||  |  ||  |
H — C — C — C — C — C — H
    |     |     |
    H     H     H
```

UNIT 7

Names and Structures of Hydrocarbons

Name the following hydrocarbons. Be sure to follow the rules when naming each compound.

1.

```
        H
        |
    H—C—H
        |
    H   H   H   H
    |   |   |   |
    C=C—C—C—C—H
    |   |   |   |
    H   |   H   H
        |
    H—C—H
        |
        H
```

2.

```
            H
            |
        H—C—H
            |
            H
            |
    H—C≡C—C—C—H
            |   |
            |   H
            |
        H—C—H
            |
            H
```

_____   _____

Draw the structural formula for each of the following hydrocarbons.

3. 1-pentyne

4. 2-methyl-3-hexene

5. 2-bromo-4-chloroheptane [Hint: the prefixes *bromo-* and *chloro-* refer to elements that are attached as side chains.]

UNIT 7

Names and Structures of Compounds with Functional Groups

Name the following organic compounds. Be sure to follow the rules when naming each compound.

1.
```
      H   H   H   O   H
      |   |   |   ||  |
  H — C — C — C — C — C — H
      |   |   |       |
      H   H   H       H
```
_____

2.
```
      H   H   OH  H   H   H
      |   |   |   |   |   |
  H — C — C — C — C — C — C — H
      |   |   |   |   |   |
      H   H   H   H   H   H
```
_____

3.
```
      H   H   H   O
      |   |   |   ||
  H — C — C — C — C — OH
      |   |   |
      H   H   H
```
_____

Draw the structural formulas for each of the following organic compounds.

4. 1,2,3-propanetriol

5. 2,2-dichloro-1,1-difluoropropane

UNIT 7 Substitution and Addition Reactions

> A substitution reaction is a reaction where one or more atoms replace another atom or group of atoms in a molecule. An addition reaction occurs when an atom or molecule is added to an unsaturated molecule.

1. Explain why alkanes do not undergo addition reactions but do participate in substitution reactions.

_____

_____

_____

_____

_____

_____

2. Under the proper conditions, propyne can react with hydrogen gas to form an alkane. Draw the structural formulas for the reactants and the product formed in this addition reaction.

3. When 2-methylpropene reacts with HI, 2-iodo-2-methylpropane is produced.

a. Draw the structural formula for the organic reactant.

b. Draw the structural formula for the organic product.

c. What type of reaction does this

represent? _____

4. Examine the following addition reaction.

$+ 3H_2 \longrightarrow$ cyclohexane

The product in this reaction is cyclohexane, an organic compound that is used to make nylon, paints, varnishes, and oils. Draw the structural formula for cyclohexane.

UNIT 7

Condensation and Hydrolysis Reactions

> *In a condensation reaction, two molecules combine, usually with the loss of a water molecule. In a hydrolysis reaction, a water molecule is added, and the bond between two monomers is broken. Hydrolysis is the reverse of the condensation reaction.*

1. Draw the structural formula of the organic product formed in a condensation reaction involving the following two reactants.

glucose   **fructose**

2. Draw the structural formulas for the products that are formed from the hydrolysis of the following organic molecule.

3. Nylon is made in a condensation reaction from two organic compounds called hexanediamine and adipic acid. The structural formulas for these two reactants are shown below.

$$H-N-CH_2-CH_2-CH_2-CH_2-CH_2-CH_2-N-H \ + \ HO-C-CH_2-CH_2-CH_2-CH_2-C-OH \rightarrow$$

Draw the structural formula for the polymer made in a condensation reaction involving these two organic molecules.

UNIT 7

Polymers

> **Polymers are large molecules that are formed by joining five or more smaller units called monomers.**

1. Ethylene glycol is the monomer used to make car wax in a condensation reaction. The formula for ethylene glycol is $HO-CH_2-CH_2-OH$. Draw the structural formula for the organic product that forms when two ethylene glycol molecules combine.

2. Polymethylmethacrylate, used to make Plexiglass®, is an addition polymer made from the monomer methyl methacrylate, whose structural formula is shown below.

Draw a portion of the polymer showing two monomers that have combined.

3. A polymer known as Kevlar® is used to make bulletproof vests. This polymer is made from the following monomer.

Draw a portion of the Kevlar® polymer showing four of the monomers above that have combined.

Chemical reactions involve the electrons of atoms. However, the nuclei of many atoms also react. The nuclei of these atoms are unstable and spontaneously break apart. In some cases, nuclei of atoms combine to produce a larger atom. Both processes are examples of nuclear changes. Nuclear changes are easier to understand than chemical changes because only a few types of nuclear changes occur.

Radioactive Decay

One type of nuclear change is the spontaneous change of an unstable nucleus to form a more stable one. This change is called radioactive decay, or **radioactivity**. Radioactivity is a nuclear change that involves the release of particles or energy in the form of electromagnetic waves, or both.

Radioactivity can involve the release of an **alpha particle**. The symbol for an alpha particle is usually written either as α, the Greek letter alpha, or as $^{4}_{2}He$. The latter symbol indicates that an alpha particle is composed of two protons and two neutrons, just like the nucleus of a helium atom. With two protons, the charge on an alpha particle is 2^{+}. The following equation shows how the nucleus of a uranium-238 atom breaks apart to produce an atom of thorium-234 by emitting an alpha particle.

$$^{238}_{92}U \xrightarrow{\text{alpha decay}} \ ^{234}_{90}Th + \ ^{4}_{2}He$$

Radioactivity can also involve the release of a **beta particle**. The symbol for a beta particle is usually written either as β, the Greek letter beta, or as $^{0}_{-1}e$. The latter symbol indicates that a beta particle is an electron and therefore has a 1- charge. The following equation shows how a carbon-14 atom emits a beta particle to produce an atom of nitrogen-14.

$$^{14}_{6}C \longrightarrow \ ^{14}_{7}N + \ ^{0}_{-1}e$$

Key Terms

radioactivity—a nuclear change that involves the release of particles or energy in the form of electromagnetic waves, or both

alpha particle—a positively charged atom that is released in the disintegration of radioactive elements and that consists of two protons and two neutrons

beta particle—a charged electron emitted during certain types of radioactive decay, such as beta decay

positron—an antiparticle of an electron released during radioactive decay

gamma rays—the high-energy waves that are emitted during a nuclear decay process

nuclear fission—a type of nuclear change that occurs when a very heavy nucleus splits into two smaller nuclei

chain reaction—a reaction where the particle that starts the reaction is also a product of the reaction; the reaction will continue until there are no unstable nuclei remaining

nuclear fusion—a nuclear change that occurs when small nuclei combine, or fuse, to form a larger, more stable nucleus

half-life—the time required for half of a sample of radioactive substance to disintegrate

radioactive dating—the process used to date an object, given the half-life

Another type of radioactivity involves the release of a **positron**. The symbol for a positron is usually written either as β^+ or as $_{+1}^{0}e$. The latter symbol indicates that a positron is an antiparticle of an electron, as indicated by the 1+ charge. The following equation shows how an atom of chromium-49 forms an atom of vanadium-49 by emitting a positron.

$$_{24}^{49}\text{Cr} \longrightarrow {}_{23}^{49}\text{V} + {}_{+1}^{0}e$$

When an unstable nucleus decays, it often also releases energy in the form of high-energy electromagnetic waves. The symbol for this energy is written as γ, the Greek letter gamma. This symbol represents the **gamma rays**, or the high-energy waves emitted during a nuclear decay process. The following equation shows that carbon-14 emits gamma rays in addition to a beta particle when it forms nitrogen-14.

$$_{6}^{14}\text{C} \longrightarrow {}_{7}^{14}\text{N} + {}_{-1}^{0}e + \gamma$$

If you look at all the nuclear equations that have appeared so far, you will notice that they are balanced. Like chemical equations, nuclear equations must also be balanced. Nuclear equations are balanced so that the sum of the mass numbers (superscripts) on one side of the equation always equals the sum of the mass numbers on the other side of the equation. Likewise, the sums of the atomic numbers or nuclear charges (subscripts) on each side are equal. For example, the following nuclear equation is balanced for both mass and nuclear charge.

$$_{92}^{238}\text{U} \longrightarrow {}_{90}^{234}\text{Th} + {}_{2}^{4}\text{He} \quad \begin{array}{l} [238 = 234 + 4 \text{ mass balance}] \\ [92 = 90 + 2 \text{ charge balance}] \end{array}$$

Fission and Fusion

One type of nuclear change you have examined is radioactivity in which a nucleus decays by either losing or adding a particle. Another type of nuclear change is called **nuclear fission**. Nuclear fission occurs when a very heavy nucleus splits into two smaller nuclei. Each smaller nucleus is more stable than the original nucleus. Some fission reactions occur spontaneously. Others are made to happen by

bombarding a nucleus with neutrons. The following equation is an example of a nuclear fission that occurs when an atom of uranium-235 is bombarded with a neutron.

$$_{92}^{235}\text{U} + {}_{0}^{1}n \xrightarrow{\text{nuclear fission}} {}_{36}^{93}\text{Kr} + {}_{56}^{140}\text{Ba} + 3{}_{0}^{1}n$$

Notice that the products include two smaller nuclei, Kr-93 and Ba-140, and three neutrons. These neutrons can then bombard additional uranium-235 nuclei to create a **chain reaction**. A characteristic of a chain reaction is that the particle that starts the reaction, in this case a neutron, is also a product of the reaction. The chain reaction will continue until there are no unstable nuclei remaining. A chain reaction can also be controlled as is the case in a nuclear reactor.

Another type of nuclear change is called **nuclear fusion**. This change occurs when small nuclei combine, or fuse, to form a larger, more stable nucleus. Fusion involves the release of a tremendous quantity of energy. Fusion is the process by which stars, including our sun, release energy. The following equation shows the fusion of four hydrogen atoms, as it occurs in our sun.

$$4{}_{1}^{1}\text{H} \longrightarrow {}_{2}^{4}\text{He} + 2{}_{+1}^{0}e.$$

Half-Lives

Unstable nuclei decay at a constant rate. This rate of decay is measured in terms of its **half-life**. A half-life is the time required for half of a sample of radioactive substance to disintegrate. For example, the half-life of carbon-14 is 5,715 years. Assume that you have a 10.0 g sample of carbon-14. In 5,715 years, only 5.0 g of carbon-14 will remain. In another 5,715 years, 2.5 g of carbon-14 will remain, and so on.

The half-life of a radioactive isotope can be used to date an object. This process is called **radioactive dating**. Carbon-14 is often used for radioactive dating. Nearly all the carbon on Earth is present as the stable carbon-12 isotope. A small percentage is made up by the unstable carbon-14. All living things have the same ratio of carbon-14 to carbon-12.

However, when an organism dies, carbon-14 decays into carbon-12, changing this ratio. Scientists can determine the age of a specimen by comparing its carbon-14 to carbon-12 ratio to that of a specimen whose age is known.

Knowing the half-life of a radioactive isotope and the ratio of unstable to stable isotope, you can determine the age of a specimen. For example, assume that a specimen has a ratio of carbon-14 to carbon-12 that is one-sixteenth the ratio of carbon-14 to carbon-12 found in a modern-day object. To have a ratio that is one-sixteenth, four half-lives must have passed.

$$\frac{1}{2} \times \frac{1}{2} \times \frac{1}{2} \times \frac{1}{2} = \frac{1}{16}$$

Therefore, the age of this object can be calculated by multiplying the number of half-lives that have passed by the half-life of carbon-14.

4 half-lives × 5715 years/half-life = 22860 years

You can also determine the amount of a radioactive isotope that was originally present in a sample. In this case, you need to know the age of the sample, the half-life of the radioactive isotope, and the quantity of radioactive isotope it contains. For example assume that a rock is 3.84 billion years old and contains 4.3 mg of potassium-40, which has a half-life of 1.28 billion years. In this example, three half-lives have passed.

3.84 billion years/1.28 billion years = 3 half-lives

For each half-life that has passed, the rock would contain half of the radioactive isotope that was originally present. In this example, you would calculate how much radioactive isotope was originally present by doubling the amount now present three times.

4.3 mg × 2 = 8.6 mg

8.6 mg × 2 = 17 mg

17 mg × 2 = 34 mg were originally present

UNIT 8

Review

Darken the circle by the best answer.

1. The symbol for an electron is also used to represent a(n)

   Ⓐ alpha particle.

   Ⓑ beta particle.

   Ⓒ positron.

   Ⓓ gamma ray.

2. Which of the following nuclear equations is correctly balanced?

   Ⓐ $^{37}_{18}\text{Ar} + ^{0}_{-1}e \rightarrow ^{37}_{17}\text{Cl}$

   Ⓑ $^{6}_{3}\text{Li} + 2^{1}_{0}n \rightarrow ^{4}_{2}\text{He} + ^{3}_{1}\text{H}$

   Ⓒ $^{254}_{99}\text{Es} + ^{4}_{2}\text{He} \rightarrow ^{258}_{101}\text{Md} + 2^{1}_{0}n$

   Ⓓ $^{14}_{7}\text{N} + ^{4}_{2}\text{He} \rightarrow ^{17}_{8}\text{O} + ^{2}_{1}\text{H}$

3. During a fission reaction

   Ⓐ a larger, more stable nucleus is formed.

   Ⓑ energy is absorbed.

   Ⓒ positrons are always released.

   Ⓓ smaller, more stable nuclei are formed.

4. A fusion reaction between a nucleus of curium-246 and carbon-12 will produce a nucleus of

   Ⓐ fermium-254.

   Ⓑ californium-252.

   Ⓒ mendelevium-256.

   Ⓓ nobelium-258.

5. The half-life of a radioactive isotope

   Ⓐ changes over time.

   Ⓑ is constant.

   Ⓒ is a characteristic of stable isotopes.

   Ⓓ decreases in value as time passes.

6. Radioactive dating is used to determine the

   Ⓐ half-life of a radioactive isotope.

   Ⓑ type of particle emitted by an isotope as it decays.

   Ⓒ age of a specimen.

   Ⓓ time required for half of a radioactive sample to decay.

7. How are an alpha particle and a helium nucleus alike?

   _____

8. Explain how fission differs from fusion. How are these two processes alike?

   _____

   _____

   _____

   _____

UNIT 8

Nuclear Equations

Complete the following nuclear equations so that they are balanced for both mass and nuclear charge. They are balanced when the values of both the superscripts and subscripts on both sides of the equation are equal.

1. $^{212}_{84}Po \rightarrow ? + ^{208}_{82}Pb$ _____

2. $^{234}_{90}Th \rightarrow ^{0}_{-1}e + ?$ _____

3. $^{142}_{61}Pm + ? \rightarrow ^{142}_{60}Nd$ _____

4. $^{253}_{99}Es + ^{4}_{2}He \rightarrow ^{1}_{0}n + ?$ _____

5. $^{236}_{92}U \rightarrow ^{94}_{36}Kr + 3^{1}_{0}n + ?$ Hint: Check the coefficient. _____

6. $^{235}_{92}U + ^{1}_{0}n \rightarrow ^{146}_{57}La + ^{87}_{35}Br + 3?$ _____

Write a balanced equation for each of the following nuclear changes. You must supply the missing product in each equation.

7. Neptunium-239 emits a beta particle.

_____

8. Sodium-22 combines with a beta particle.

_____

9. Uranium-238 emits an alpha particle.

_____

10. Four hydrogen-1 nuclei combine and release two positrons.

_____

UNIT 8

Fission and Fusion

> *Fission is a type of nuclear change that occurs when a very heavy nucleus splits into two smaller nuclei. Fusion occurs when small nuclei combine, or fuse, to form a larger, more stable nucleus.*

When an atom of uranium-235 is bombarded with a neutron, several different fission reactions are possible. Write the balanced nuclear equation for each of the fission reactions. Each equation must be balanced for both mass and nuclear charge.

1. The uranium-235 nucleus breaks apart to form a cesium-144 nucleus and a rubidium-90 nucleus.

_____

2. The uranium-235 nucleus undergoes fission to produce a bromine-87 nucleus and a lanthanum-146 nucleus.

_____

3. Write the balanced equation for the nuclear reaction that occurs when a neon-21 nucleus is bombarded with an alpha particle (helium nucleus) and forms a magnesium-24 nucleus. Is this an example of a fission or fusion reaction? Explain your answer.

_____

_____

4. A fusion reaction that occurs in the sun involves the combination of two helium-3 nuclei. The products include two hydrogen nuclei and one other nucleus. Write the balanced nuclear equation for this reaction.

_____

5. In addition to uranium-235, nuclear reactors also use plutonium-239 as a fuel. The first step in a series of fission reactions involving plutonium-239 is the release of an alpha particle (helium nucleus). Write the nuclear equation for this reaction.

_____

6. Write the balanced nuclear equation for the fusion reaction between a lead-208 nucleus and an iron-58 nucleus. One of the two products is a neutron.

_____

_____

Half-Life Problems

UNIT 8

A half-life is the time required for half of a sample of radioactive substance to disintegrate. After two half-lives, one-quarter of the original sample will remain, and so on.

---

1. The half-life of thorium-234 is 24.1 days. How much time must pass for one-eighth of a given amount of this radioactive isotope to remain?

_____

2. Assume that you have 16 mg of iodine-131. How much time must pass for only 0.5 mg to remain? The half-life of iodine-131 is 8.02 days.

_____

3. Calculate the age of a fossil that contains 1/128 of the ratio of carbon-14 to carbon-12 found in a living thing today.

_____

4. The half-life of radium-224 is 3.66 days. What was the original mass of this radioactive isotope if 1.2 mg remains after 10.98 days?

_____

5. Potassium-40 was used to date moon rocks. The half life of this radioactive isotope is 1.28×10^9 years. The oldest lunar rocks were found to be 4.5 billion years old. Approximately how many half-lives has potassium-40 passed through in these rocks?

_____

6. In 1978, a 200-gram sample of cobalt-60 was buried in the Yucca Mountains, just northwest of Las Vegas, Nevada. How much of this sample was present in 2004? The half-life of cobalt-60 is 5.23 years.

_____

UNIT 8 — Nuclear Chemistry Puzzle

Use the clues to unscramble the letters to form a word. Then, unscramble all the circled letters to get the answer to the question.

1. sinosif—breaking apart of a large nucleus

__ Ⓞ __ __ __ Ⓞ __

2. falshevil—5715 years for carbon-14 and only 8.02 days for iodine-131

__ Ⓞ __ __ __ Ⓞ Ⓞ __ __

3. cadey—what radioactive isotopes naturally do

Ⓞ __ __ Ⓞ

4. dancelab—how all nuclear equations must be

__ Ⓞ __ __ __ __ __ __

5. tarpallaphice— $^4_2$He

__ __ __ __ __ __ __ __ Ⓞ __ Ⓞ __ __

6. mulehi—the sun makes it by fusion

__ __ __ Ⓞ __ __

7. tripsoon—electron with a positive charges

__ __ __ __ Ⓞ Ⓞ __ __

8. Word that some people find frightening

__ __ __ __ __ __ __ __ __ __ __

UNIT 9

Oxidation and Reduction

You learned that some atoms bond by transferring electrons. For example, consider a potassium atom that gives up its valence electron, which is then taken by a chlorine atom. Both potassium and chlorine form ions that join by forming an ionic bond. Covalent bonds are formed by a sharing of electrons. However, this sharing is often unequal so that the electrons are more strongly attracted by one of the atoms in the compound. For example, carbon and oxygen react to form carbon monoxide by sharing electrons. The shared electrons are attracted more strongly by the oxygen atom. In this case, the carbon atom has not totally lost an electron but does give it up at times. The loss and gain, either wholly or in part, of electrons make up a particular type of chemical reaction.

Redox Reactions

The loss, either wholly or in part, of an electron is called **oxidation**. An atom that undergoes oxidation is said to be oxidized. Therefore, both K and C are oxidized when they form the bonds described above.

In contrast, the gain, either wholly or in part, of an electron is called **reduction**. An atom that undergoes reduction is said to be reduced. Therefore, both Cl and O are reduced when they form the bonds described above.

An atom cannot be oxidized unless another atom is reduced. In other words, oxidation and reduction must happen simultaneously. A single reaction in which oxidation and reduction occur is called an **oxidation-reduction reaction**, or simply a redox reaction. In a redox reaction, the substance oxidized is also the reducing agent. The substance reduced is

Key Terms

oxidation—the loss, either wholly or in part, of an electron

reduction—the gain, either wholly or in part, of an electron

oxidation-reduction reaction—a single reaction in which oxidation and reduction occur simultaneously

oxidation number—the number of electrons that must be either removed or added to an atom in the combined state to change the atom into the elemental form

activity series—a list of elements organized according to the ease with which the elements undergo certain reactions, such as a redox reaction

electrochemical cell—a system that contains two electrodes separated by an electrolyte phase

electrode—a conductor used to establish electrical contact with a nonmetallic part of a circuit, such as an electrolyte

anode—the electrode on whose surface oxidation takes place; anions migrate toward the anode, and electrons leave the system from the anode

cathode—the electrode on whose surface reduction takes place

electrolytic cell—an electrochemical device in which electrical energy is used to bring about a chemical change

also the oxidizing agent. For example, again consider the reaction between potassium and chlorine.

$$2K + Cl_2 \rightarrow 2KCl$$

In the reaction above, K is oxidized and serves as the reducing agent. In contrast, Cl_2 is reduced and serves as the oxidizing agent.

Oxidation Numbers

One way to determine if a reaction is a redox reaction is with the help of **oxidation numbers**. An oxidation number is the number of electrons that must be either removed or added to an atom in the combined state to change the atom into the elemental form. Certain rules are followed to assign an oxidation number to an element.

1. The oxidation number of any uncombined element is zero.
2. The oxidation number of a monatomic ion is equal to the charge on the ion.
3. In compounds, atoms of Group 1, Group 2, and aluminum have oxidation numbers of $+1$, $+2$, and $+3$, respectively.
4. The oxidation number of hydrogen in a compound is $+1$, unless it is combined with a metal atom; then it is -1.
5. The oxidation number of fluorine in a compound is always -1.
6. The oxidation number of oxygen is -2, except with compounds of fluorine where it is $+2$ and in peroxides such as H_2O_2 where it is -1.
7. The sum of all oxidations numbers in a compound is zero.
8. The sum of all oxidation numbers in a polyatomic ion equals the charge on that ion.

For example, consider the oxidation numbers of HSO_3^-: H: $+1$; S: $+4$; O: -2. Each O atom has an oxidation number of -2 while the total charge is -6. Because the oxidation number of H is $+1$ and the charge on this polyatomic ion is -1, then the S atom must have an oxidation number of $+4$.

You can identify a redox reaction by comparing the oxidation numbers of all atoms in the reactants and products. In a redox reaction, the oxidation

number of an atom that is oxidized increases, while that of an atom that is reduced decreases. Consider the following reaction.

$$H_2 + Cl_2 \rightarrow 2HCl$$

Use the rules above to assign oxidation numbers.

$$\overset{0}{H_2} + \overset{0}{Cl_2} \rightarrow 2\overset{+1\,-1}{HCl}$$

Notice that the oxidation number of H has changed from 0 to $+1$. Therefore, H has been oxidized. In contrast, Cl has been reduced because its oxidation number decreased from 0 to -1.

Activity Series

You learned about other types of chemical reactions, including single-replacement reactions. The following is an example of a single-replacement reaction.

$$2Al + 3Pb(NO_3)_2 \rightarrow 3Pb + 2Al(NO_3)_3$$

Recall that the reaction above is called a single-replacement reaction because Al replaces Pb. If you check the oxidation numbers of the atoms in the reaction above, you will notice that it is also an example of a redox reaction. All single-replacement reactions are also redox reactions. However, the fact that a single-replacement reaction can be written does not mean that the reaction takes place. For example, consider what happens when cobalt is placed in a solution of sodium chloride.

$$Co + NaCl \rightarrow \text{no reaction}$$

Cobalt cannot replace sodium. As a result, this is neither an example of a single-replacement reaction nor a redox reaction. To determine if such a reaction will occur, you must refer to an **activity series**. An activity series is a list of elements organized according to the ease with which the elements undergo certain reactions, such as a redox reaction. The most active element is placed at the top. Any element can replace each of the elements below it from a compound in a single-replacement reaction. However, an element farther down cannot replace an element above it on the activity series. The following is an activity series.

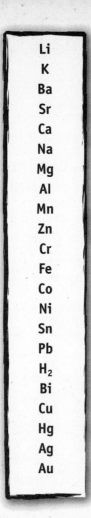

Li
K
Ba
Sr
Ca
Na
Mg
Al
Mn
Zn
Cr
Fe
Co
Ni
Sn
Pb
H₂
Bi
Cu
Hg
Ag
Au

Notice that Co is below Na. Therefore, Co cannot replace Na from a compound. However, the following redox reaction does occur spontaneously.

$$Co + CuSO_4 \rightarrow Cu + CoSO_4$$

Electrochemical Cells

Electrochemistry is the study of the connections between chemistry and electricity. One practical application of electrochemistry is a flashlight battery, which converts chemical energy into electrical energy, which is then converted into light energy. A battery is an example of an **electrochemical cell**. An electrochemical cell consists of two **electrodes** separated by an electrolyte. An electrode is a conductor that connects with a nonmetallic part of an electrical circuit. An electrolyte is a substance that dissolves in water to produce a solution that conducts electricity.

Inside a battery, spontaneous redox reactions occur that cause electrons to move. This movement or flow of electrons produces an electrical current. To

understand how a battery operates to change chemical energy into electrical energy, examine the following diagram.

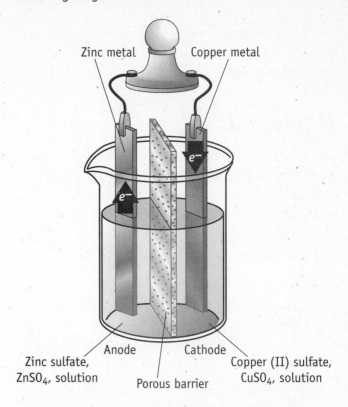

Zinc metal   Copper metal

e⁻

e⁻

Anode   Cathode
Zinc sulfate,   Copper (II) sulfate,
ZnSO₄, solution   CuSO₄, solution
Porous barrier

Zinc atoms lose electrons that flow through the wire connected to the bulb. The zinc metal serves as an electrode where oxidation, or loss of electrons, occurs. This electrode is called the **anode**. The flow of electrons through the wire produces the electricity that lights the bulb. The electrons then flow to the copper metal. Copper ions in solution are reduced by gaining electrons at the **cathode**. These copper ions form copper atoms that gradually collect on the copper metal.

Most car batteries contain solutions like the electrochemical cell shown in the illustration above. However, flashlight batteries do not use solutions. Rather they use moist electrolyte pastes and are therefore known as dry cells.

Electrolytic Cells

The activity series is useful in determining if a redox reaction will occur spontaneously. Such spontaneous redox reactions are the basis of electrochemical cells. In contrast, nonspontaneous redox reactions are the basis of **electrolytic cells**. An electrolytic cell is a

Unit 9, Oxidation and Reduction
Chemistry, SV 0424-7

device in which electrical energy is used to bring about a chemical change. To understand how an electrolytic cell operates, examine the following illustration.

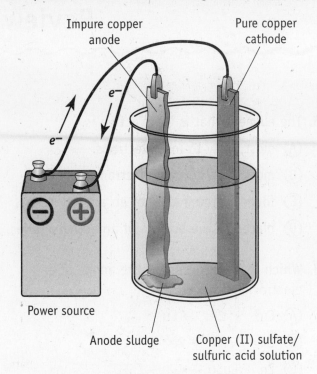

Impure copper anode

Pure copper cathode

e⁻

e⁻

e⁻

Power source

Anode sludge

Copper (II) sulfate/ sulfuric acid solution

Notice that a battery is connected to the electrodes to supply the electrical energy needed to bring about the chemical changes. Oxidation occurs at the anode where Cu atoms in the impure copper are changed to Cu^{2+} ions. In turn, these Cu^{2+} ions are reduced at the cathode to form Cu atoms. These Cu atoms are added to the pure copper cathode. This is how copper is refined.

Unit 9, Oxidation and Reduction
Chemistry, SV 0424-7

UNIT 9

Review

Darken the circle by the best answer.

1. An atom that is oxidized
   - (A) gains one or more electrons.
   - (B) loses one or more electrons.
   - (C) does not change its oxidation number.
   - (D) also serves as an oxidizing agent.

2. The oxidation number of the Mn atom in Mn_2O_3 is
   - (A) −2.
   - (B) −6.
   - (C) +2.
   - (D) +3.

3. Which is an example of a redox reaction?
   - (A) $H_2SO_4 + 2KOH \rightarrow K_2SO_4 + 2H_2O$
   - (B) $NaCl + AgNO_3 \rightarrow AgCl + NaNO_3$
   - (C) $2HNO_3 + 3H_2S \rightarrow 2NO + 4H_2O + 3S$
   - (D) $2NH_4Cl + Ca(OH)_2 \rightarrow 2NH_3 + 2H_2O + CaCl_2$

4. Which element can replace Ni in a redox reaction?
   - (A) Fe
   - (B) Pb
   - (C) Ag
   - (D) Cu

5. The element that is least active is
   - (A) most likely to lose electrons.
   - (B) most likely to gain electrons.
   - (C) found in the middle of an activity series.
   - (D) placed at the bottom of an activity series.

6. Which reaction occurs at the anode of an electrochemical cell?
   - (A) $Cu^{2+} + 2e^- \rightarrow Cu$
   - (B) $Zn \rightarrow Zn^{2+} + 2e^-$
   - (C) $Zn + CuSO_4 \rightarrow Cu + ZnSO_4$
   - (D) $Zn^{2+} + 2e^- \rightarrow Zn$

7. An electrolytic cell differs from an electrochemical cell in that the electrolytic cell
   - (A) involves a redox reaction.
   - (B) is spontaneous.
   - (C) generates electrical energy.
   - (D) requires an external electric current.

8. How does oxidation differ from reduction?

   _____

   _____

9. What is an electrochemical cell?

   _____

   _____

   _____

   _____

UNIT 9

Oxidation Numbers

> *An oxidation number is the number of electrons that must be either removed or added to an atom in the combined state to change the atom into the elemental form.*

Assign an oxidation number to each atom in the following. Certain rules must be followed when assigning an oxidation number to an element.

1. Au

_____

2. H_2O

_____

3. Mg^{2+}

_____

4. K_2O

_____

5. BF_3

_____

6. NH_4^+

_____

7. $Ca(OH)_2$

_____

8. S_2O_7

_____

9. $Fe_2(CO_3)_3$

_____

10. $NaBiO_3$

_____

11. $NaHCO_3$

_____

12. $Cr_2O_7^{2-}$

_____

13. NH_4NO_3

_____

14. $H_2PO_4^-$

_____

UNIT 9

Redox Reactions

> A redox reaction involves a change in the
> oxidation number of two or more elements.

Determine which of the following is an example of a redox reaction. For each redox reaction, identify the substance oxidized and the substance reduced.

1. $2KNO_3 \rightarrow 2KNO_2 + O_2$ _____

_____

2. $SO_2 + H_2O \rightarrow H_2SO_3$ _____

_____

3. $H_2S + 8HNO_3 \rightarrow H_2SO_4 + 8NO_2 + 4H_2O$ _____

_____

_____

4. $Zn + CuSO_4 \rightarrow ZnSO_4 + Cu$ _____

_____

5. $NH_3 + HCl \rightarrow NH_4^+ + Cl^-$ _____

_____

6. $10FeSO_4 + 2KMnO_4 + 8H_2SO_4 \rightarrow 5Fe_2(SO_4)_3 + 2MnSO_4 + K_2SO_4 + 8H_2O$ _____

_____

_____

7. $4Fe + 3O_2 + 6H_2O \rightarrow 4Fe(OH)_3$ _____

_____

_____

UNIT 9

Activity Series

> An activity series is a list of elements organized according to the ease with which the elements undergo certain reactions, such as a redox reaction.

Use an activity series to predict whether each of the following single-replacement or redox reactions will occur. For the reactions that will take place, write the products and balance the equation. Also identify the changes in oxidation numbers, the substance that is oxidized, and the substance that is reduced.

1. $Mg + Pb(NO_3)_2 \rightarrow$ _____

_____

2. $Na + H_2O \rightarrow$ _____

_____

3. $Au + CaCl_2 \rightarrow$ _____

_____

4. $Al + Zn(NO_3)_2 \rightarrow$ _____

_____

5. $Pb + Fe_2(SO_4)_3 \rightarrow$ _____

_____

6. $Mg + HCl \rightarrow$ _____

_____

7. $Ni + CuSO_4 \rightarrow$ _____

_____

_____

UNIT 9

Electrochemical Cells

> *Electrochemical cells are a system that contain two electrodes separated by an electrolyte phase.*

An alkaline battery contains potassium hydroxide, a strong base that gives the alkaline cell its name. The battery is covered by a sturdy steel shell to prevent the caustic contents from leaking out. This extra packing makes an alkaline cell more expensive than an acid battery.

> The following is one of the redox reactions that occur in an alkaline battery.
> $$2MnO_2 + H_2O \rightarrow Mn_2O_3 + 2OH^-$$

1. Assign oxidation numbers to each atom in this reaction.

_____

_____

2. Which element is involved in the redox reaction?

_____

3. Does this reaction occur at the anode or at the cathode? Explain your answer.

_____

_____

_____

4. Explain what will happen to MnO_2 over time.

_____

_____

_____

Electrochemical Cells (cont'd.)

> **The following is the other redox reaction that occurs in an alkaline battery.**
>
> $Zn + OH^- \rightarrow Zn(OH)_2$

5. Assign oxidation numbers to each atom in this reaction.

_____

_____

6. Which element is involved in the redox reaction?

_____

7. Does this reaction occur at the anode or at the cathode? Explain your answer.

_____

_____

_____

8. Explain what will happen to the zinc over time.

_____

_____

_____

UNIT 9

Electrolytic Cells

An electrolytic cell is used to plate an object with a metal. This process is called electroplating. Forks, spoons, and jewelry are often electroplated to give them a shiny appearance. For example, the following illustration shows how a bracelet is electroplated with silver.

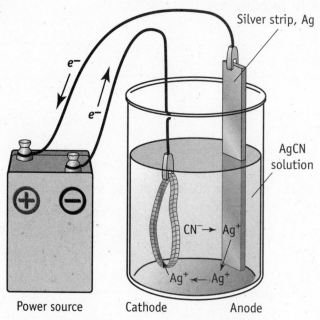

1. Write the redox reaction that occurs at the anode. Be sure to show how electrons are involved.

_____

_____

2. Write the redox reaction that occurs at the cathode. Be sure to show how electrons are involved.

_____

_____

3. Explain why a battery is connected to the bracelet and silver strip.

_____

_____

_____

4. What happens to the silver strip as the electrolytic cell continues to operate?

_____

_____

_____

_____

5. Explain why the process illustrated above is called electroplating.

_____

_____

_____

_____

_____

Unit 9, Oxidation and Reduction
Chemistry, SV 0424-7

GLOSSARY

activated complex—a molecule in an unstable state intermediate to the reactants and the products in the chemical reaction (p. 44)

activation energy—the minimum energy required to start a chemical reaction (p. 44)

activity series—a list of elements organized according to the ease with which the elements undergo certain reactions, such as a redox reaction (p. 101)

addition reaction—a type of chemical reaction where an atom or molecule is added to an unsaturated molecule (p. 81)

alkanes—the simplest hydrocarbons which consist of carbon atoms that are connected only by single bonds (p. 79)

alkenes—hydrocarbons which consist of at least one double bond between two carbon atoms (p. 80)

alkynes—hydrocarbons which consist of at least one triple bond between two carbon atoms (p. 80)

alpha particle—a positively charged atom that is released in the disintegration of radioactive elements and that consists of two protons and two neutrons (p. 92)

anion—an ion that has accepted an electron, producing a negative charge (p. 30)

anode—the electrode on whose surface oxidation takes place; anions migrate toward the anode, and electrons leave the system from the anode (p. 102)

atomic mass—the unit used to express the mass of an atom or the mass of a subatomic particle (p. 18)

atomic number—the number of protons an atom has (p. 18)

atom—the smallest unit of an element that retains all the properties of that element (p. 17)

average atomic mass—a weighted average of the atomic masses of all the isotopes of an element (p. 18)

Avogadro's number—the value associated with the number of atoms of carbon in exactly one mole of carbon-12 (6.02×10^{23} units/mol) (p. 55)

beta particle—a charged electron emitted during certain types of radioactive decay, such as beta decay (p. 92)

Brønsted-Lowry acid—a substance that donates a proton to another substance (p. 70)

Brønsted-Lowry base—a substance that accepts a proton from another substance (p. 70)

cathode—the electrode on whose surface reduction takes place (p. 102)

cation—an ion that has given up an electron, producing a positive charge (p. 30)

chain reaction—a reaction where the particle that starts the reaction is also a product of the reaction; the reaction will continue until there are no unstable nuclei remaining (p. 93)

chemical change—a change that occurs when one or more substances change into entirely new substances with different properties (p. 6)

chemical reaction—the process by which one or more substances change into one or more new substances (p. 42)

combustion reaction—a reaction involving a carbon-based compound reacting with oxygen (p. 43)

compound—a substance made up of atoms of two or more different elements joined by chemical bonds (p. 5)

condensation reaction—a reaction where two molecules combine, usually with the loss of a water molecule (p. 82)

conjugate acid—an acid that forms when a base gains a proton (p. 70)

conjugate base—an base that forms when an acid loses a proton (p. 70)

GLOSSARY

covalent bond—a bond formed when atoms share one or more pairs of electrons (p. 29)

decomposition reaction—a reaction where a single compound breaks down into two or more elements or simpler compounds (p. 43)

double covalent bond—a covalent bond formed by sharing two pairs of electrons (p. 30)

double-displacement reaction—a reaction where two compounds appear to exchange ions and form two new compounds (p. 43)

effusion—the passage of a gas under pressure through a tiny opening (p. 57)

electrochemical cell—a system that contains two electrodes separated by an electrolyte phase (p. 102)

electrode—a conductor used to establish electrical contact with a nonmetallic part of a circuit, such as an electolyte (p. 102)

electrolyte—a substance that conducts electricity when present in a solution (p. 69)

electrolytic cell—an electrochemical device in which electrical energy is used to bring about a chemical change (p. 102)

electron—a subatomic particle that has a negative charge, usually written as −1 (p. 18)

electron configuration—the description of how an atom's electrons orbit its nucleus (p. 19)

electronegativity—a measure of the ability of an atom in a chemical compound to attract electrons (p. 20)

element—a substance that cannot be separated or broken down into simpler substances by ordinary means (p. 5)

elimination reaction—a reaction where a simple molecule, such as water or ammonia, is removed from a compound to produce a new substance (p. 82)

empirical formula—a chemical formula that shows the composition of a compound in terms of the relative numbers and kinds of atoms in the simplest ratio (p. 55)

endothermic process—a process in which heat is absorbed from the environment (p. 6)

excited state—a state in which an electron has more energy than it does at its ground state (p. 19)

exothermic process—a process in which a substance releases heat into the environment (p. 6)

functional group—the portion of a molecule that is active in a chemical reaction and that determines the properties of many organic compounds (p. 80)

gamma rays—the high-energy waves that are emitted during a nuclear decay process (p. 93)

ground state—the state in which an electron has the lowest energy level available (p. 19)

group—a vertical column in the periodic table (p. 20)

half-life—the time required for half of a sample of radioactive substance to disintegrate (p. 93)

heat—the energy transferred between objects that are at different temperatures (p. 4)

hydrocarbon—an organic compound composed only of hydrogen and carbon (p. 79)

hydrolysis reaction—a reaction where a water molecule is added and the bond between two monomers is broken (p. 82)

ideal gas law—a law which relates all four gas variables, including pressure, volume, and the number of moles of a gas, written as $PV=nRT$ (p. 57)

ion—an atom that has gained or lost one or more electrons and has a negative or positive charge (p. 20)

ionic bond—a bond that forms when one atom gives up one or more electrons to another atom (p. 30)

GLOSSARY

ionization energy—the energy required to remove an electron from an atom (p. 20)

isomer—one of two or more compounds that have the same chemical composition but different structures (p. 80)

isotopes—atoms of the same element that have different numbers of neutrons (p. 18)

kinetic energy—the movement of particles (p. 4)

law of conservation of energy—a law that states that energy can only be transformed from one form to another, not created or destroyed (p. 44)

law of conservation of mass—a law that states that the total mass of the products equals the total mass of the reactants (p. 42)

Lewis structure—a structural formula in which electrons are represented as dots; dot pairs or dashes between two atomic symbols represent pairs in covalent bonds (p. 31)

mass—the amount of matter in an object or substance (p. 3)

mass number—the total number of protons and neutrons of the nucleus (p. 18)

matter—anything that has mass and takes up space (p. 3)

mixture—a combination of two or more substances that are not chemically combined (p. 6)

molarity—the concentration unit of a solution expressed as moles of solute dissolved per liter of solution (p. 56)

mole—the number of atoms of carbon in exactly 12 grams of carbon-12 (p. 54)

molecular formula—a chemical formula that shows the number and kinds of atoms in a molecule, but not the arrangement of the atoms (p. 56)

neutron—a subatomic particle that is neutral (p. 18)

nonpolar covalent bond—a covalent bond in which the bonding electrons are equally attracted to both bonded atoms (p. 30)

normality—the molarity of the solution times the number of either H_3O^+ ions or OH^- ions produced per molecule of substance (p. 71)

nuclear fission—a type of nuclear change that occurs when a very heavy nucleus splits into two smaller nuclei (p. 93)

nuclear fusion—a nuclear change that occurs when small nuclei combine, or fuse, to form a larger, more stable nucleus (p. 93)

nucleus—the central region of an atom where the protons and neutrons are located (p. 18)

organic compound—with some exceptions, any compound that contains the element carbon (p. 79)

oxidation—the loss, either wholly or in part, of an electron (p. 100)

oxidation number—the number of electrons that must be either removed or added to an atom in the combined state to change the atom into the elemental form (p. 101)

oxidation-reduction reaction—a single reaction in which oxidation and reduction occur simultaneously (p. 100)

percentage composition—the percentage by mass of each element in the compound (p. 55)

period—a horizontal row in the periodic table (p. 20)

pH—a value used to express acidity or alkalinity of a solution; it is defined as the logarithm of the reciprocal of the concentration of hydronium ions (p. 70)

physical change—a change of matter from one form to another without a change in chemical properties (p. 6)

Glossary
Chemistry, SV 0424-7

GLOSSARY

polar covalent bond—a covalent bond in which a pair of electrons shared by two atoms is held more closely by one atom (p. 30)

polyatomic ion—an ion formed when several atoms combine (p. 31)

polymer—a large molecule that is formed by joining five or more smaller units called monomers (p. 81)

positron—an antiparticle of an electron released during radioactive decay (p. 93)

proton—a subatomic particle that has a positive charge, usually written as +1 (p. 18)

radioactive dating—the process used to date an object, given the half-life (p. 93)

radioactivity—a nuclear change that involves the release of particles or energy in the form of electromagnetic waves, or both (p. 92)

reduction—the gain, either wholly or in part, of an electron (p. 100)

single covalent bond—a covalent bond between two atoms achieving stability by sharing a pair of electrons (p. 30)

single-displacement reaction—a reaction where a single element reacts with a compound and displaces another element from the compound (p. 44)

solute—a substance that is dissolved (p. 56)

solvent—the substance in which the solute is dissolved (p. 56)

stoichiometry—the proportional relationships between two or more substances during a chemical reaction (p. 54)

structural formula—a formula that shows how the atoms are arranged or connected (p. 30)

substitution reaction—a type of chemical reaction where one or more atoms replace another atom or group of atoms in a molecule (p. 81)

synthesis reaction—a reaction where two or more substances combine to form a new compound (p. 43)

temperature—a measure of how hot or cold something is (p. 4)

titration—a method to determine the concentration of a substance in solution by adding a solution of known volume and concentration until the reaction is completed (p. 71)

triple covalent bond—a covalent bond formed by sharing three pairs of electrons (p. 30)

valence electron—an electron found in the outermost shell of an atom that determines the atom's chemical properties (p. 20)

vapor pressure—the partial pressure exerted by a vapor that is in equilibrium with its liquid state at a given temperature (p. 5)

volume—a measure of the size of a body or region in three-dimensional space (p. 3)

weight—a measure of the gravitational force exerted on an object (p. 3)

Page 7

Review

1. B   2. C   3. A   4. C
5. D   6. A   7. B

8. An endothermic process absorbs energy, and an exothermic process releases energy.

9. A physical change does not involve any change in the identity of a substance. In contrast, a chemical change occurs when one or more substances change into entirely new substances with different properties.

Page 8

States of Matter

1. Model B represents a liquid because the particles are not tightly held together and therefore can move past one another.

2. The particles in model C remain in fixed positions as this model represents a solid.

3. Models A and D represent gases where the particles take the shape and volume of whatever container they occupy.

4. The volume will remain the same, but the shape will change because model B represents a liquid where the particles can move past one another.

Page 9

Heat and Temperature

1. There are two "plateaus" on the graph where no temperature increase is recorded even though energy is being added as heat.

2. The energy being added as heat increases the average kinetic energy of the liquid particles, resulting in an increase in temperature.

3. The energy being added as heat is used to move the liquid particles father apart rather than increasing their average kinetic energy. As they move apart, the particles form a gas.

4. solid and liquid

5. The freezing point would be the same as the melting point.

6. The temperature would remain constant until all the gas has condensed into a liquid.

Page 10

Liquids and Vapor Pressure

1. As the temperature increases, their vapor pressure increases.

2. liquid A

3. about 450 mm Hg

4. about 54°C

5. about 78°C

6. liquid C

7. liquids A and B

8. The temperature must decrease from about 91°C to about 86°C.

9. liquid A

10.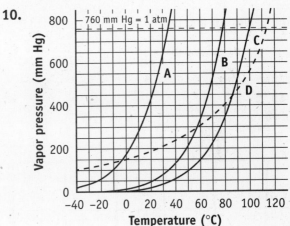

Page 11

Boyle's Law

1. As the pressure increases at constant temperature, the volume of the gas decreases as stated by Boyle's law.

2. The volume is reduced by half, from 0.500 L to 0.025 L.

3. Increasing the pressure from 100 kPa to 150 kPa causes the largest decrease in volume.

4. The volume should drop to slightly less than 0.100 L.

5. 100 kPa $\times$ 0.500 L = 550 kPa $\times$? L;
   The calculated answer is 0.091 L.

6. The values for any two points should show that $P_1V_1 = P_2V_2$. For example, (100 kPa $\times$ 0.500 L = 250 kPa $\times$ 0.200 L).

Page 12
Charles's Law

1. As the temperature increases at constant pressure, the volume of the gas increases as stated by Charles's law.

2. The volume doubles, increasing from 0.200 L to 0.400 L.

3. The volume of the gas would be 0.000 L.

4. $\dfrac{0.200 \text{ L}}{100 \text{ K}} = \dfrac{?\text{L}}{500 \text{ K}}$; The calculated answer is 1.000 L.

5. The values for any two points should show that $\dfrac{V_1}{T_1} = \dfrac{V_2}{T_2}$. For example, $\dfrac{0.200 \text{ L}}{100 \text{ K}} = \dfrac{0.400 \text{ L}}{200 \text{ K}}$

Page 13
Combined Gas Law

Note: The answers are in bold below.

P_1	V_1	T_1	P_2	V_2	T_2
600 mm Hg	24 mL	18°C	430 mm Hg	**34.2 mL**	24°C
1.7 atm	1.6 L	25°C	1.2 atm	2.2 L	10°C
95 kPa	224 mL	374 K	125 kPa	450 mL	**989 K**
760 torr	2.4 L	37°C	**370 torr**	4.8 L	300 K
1.5 atm	**1.23 L**	−20°C	2.6 atm	750 mL	−5°C

Page 14
Elements, Compounds, and Mixtures

1. element
2. homogeneous
3. pure gold
4. mixture
5. compound
6. alloy
7. heterogeneous

Page 15
Separation of Mixtures

1. Pick them out by hand.
2. Heat the liquid to evaporate the water, leaving the salts.
3. Use cheesecloth or a filter to trap the pulp.
4. Allow the mixture to settle and then pour off the top layer.
5. Use a screen to trap the pebbles.
6. Use a magnet to attract the iron filings.
7. Add the mixture to water to dissolve the salt. Filter the mixture to trap the sand. Finally, heat the liquid to recover the salt.
8. Gradually heat the bracelet. As its melting point is reached, each metal will liquefy at a different temperature.

ANSWER KEY cont'd.

9. You could pick them out based on size. However, if there are a lot, you may want to pass them through holes of increasing size.

10. Heating the mixture of iron and sulfur changed it into a compound.

Page 16
Physical and Chemical Changes

1. physical
2. physical
3. chemical
4. physical
5. chemical
6. chemical
7. chemical
8. physical
9. physical
10. chemical
11. endothermic
12. exothermic
13. exothermic
14. endothermic
15. exothermic
16. endothermic
17. exothermic
18. exothermic
19. endothermic
20. exothermic

Page 21
Review

1. D
2. B
3. C
4. C
5. A
6. B

7. Isotopes must have the same atomic numbers but different atomic masses.

8. The former represents the electron configuration in the ground state, while the latter represents an electron configuration in an excited state.

Page 22
Parts of an Atom

Atomic Symbol	Number of Protons	Number of Neutrons	Number of Electrons
$^{4}_{2}He$	2	2	2
$^{80}_{35}Br$	35	45	35
$^{11}_{5}B$	5	6	5
$^{133}_{55}Cs$	55	78	55
$^{106}_{46}Pd$	46	60	46

1. $^{197}_{79}Au$
2. 125 neutrons
3. 13 electrons
4. 64
5. $^{21}_{10}Ne$

Page 23
Isotopes and Atomic Masses

1. lead-207

2. They all have the same atomic number, and therefore, the same number of protons and electrons.

3. The atomic number of silver must also be known.

4. Isotopes must have the same atomic number, not the same mass number.

5. They are not isotopes, but rather two ways of representing the same element with an atomic number of 8 and a mass number of 16.

6.

Atomic Symbol	# of Protons	# of Neutrons	# of Electrons
$^{130}_{56}Ba$	56	74	56
$^{137}_{56}Ba$	56	81	56
$^{140}_{56}Ba$	56	84	56

7. $^{234}_{92}U$ and $^{238}_{92}U$
8. 55.9 amu

Page 24
Electron Configuration Puzzle

1. atom
2. orbit
3. energy
4. ground
5. hydrogen
6. spherical
7. excellent
8. I am so excited!

ANSWER KEY cont'd.

Page 25
Writing Electron Configurations
1. $1s^2 2s^2 2p^3$
2. $1s^2 2s^2 2p^6$
3. $1s^2 2s^2 2p^6 3s^1$
4. $3p^1$
5. $1s^2 2s^2 2p^6 3s^2 3p^6 4s^2$
6. $1s^2 2s^2 2p^5 3s^2 3p^6 4s^2 4p^1$

Page 26
The Periodic Table
1. D   2. J   3. G   4. H
5. A   6. C   7. F   8. E
9. I   10. B

Page 27
Ionization Energy: A Periodic Trend
1. K; He
2. Al and Ga
3. As you proceed across a period, the ionization energy generally increases.
4. Group 18
5. These two groups show a slight decrease in ionization energies compared to Group 12 and 15 respectively. This represents a contradiction to the statement that ionization energies increase as you proceed across a period.
6. Yes. For example H, a member of Group 1, has the same ionization energy as O, a member of group 16.
7. Group 1 or the alkali metals
8. The ionization energy of Ne is about 2.5 times greater than that of Se.

Page 28
Electronegativity: A Periodic Trend
1. F
2. As you proceed across a period, the electronegativity values generally increase.
3. Cl
4. Group 18 or the noble gases

5. Period 2
6. Group 1 or the alkali metals
7. F
8. The graph should show increasing electronegativity values plotted on the y-axis versus the elements of Period 2 plotted on the x-axis.

Page 33
Review
1. B   2. C   3. A   4. D
5. B   6. B   7. C
8. $Ti_2 (SO_4)_3$ and $CrPO_4$
9. The symbol represents the nucleus with its protons and neutrons and all the nonvalence electrons.

Page 34
Covalent Bonds
1. Cl—Cl
2. H—Cl
3. H—O—H
4.
$$H-\underset{\underset{H}{|}}{\overset{\overset{H}{|}}{C}}-H$$
5.
$$H-\underset{\underset{H}{|}}{N}-H$$
6. S=C=S
7. Cl—O—Cl
8. H—O—Cl
9.
$$\underset{\underset{H}{|}}{\overset{\overset{H}{|}}{C}}=\underset{\underset{H}{|}}{\overset{\overset{H}{|}}{C}}$$
10.
$$F-\underset{\underset{Cl}{|}}{\overset{\overset{Cl}{|}}{C}}-F$$

Page 35
Names of Covalent Compounds
1. H—Br
2.
$$F-\underset{\underset{F}{|}}{N}-F$$
3. I—Cl
4. Cl—O—Cl
5. S=C=S
6. PCl_3
7. N_2O
8. XeF_4
9. Si_3N_4
10. Np_3O_8

ANSWER KEY cont'd.

Page 36
Ionic Compounds

1. KBr
2. $MgBr_2$
3. CaO
4. Na_2O
5. K_3N
6. $AlBr_3$
7. BaS
8. Al_2S_3
9. Li_2O
10. Al_2O_3

Page 37
Polyatomic Ions

1. $NaCH_3COO$
2. $Ca(OH)_2$
3. $AlPO_4$
4. $(NH_4)_2SO_4$
5. $Li_2S_2O_3$
6. NH_4OH
7. $Al_2(CO_3)_3$
8. KNO_3
9. $Mg(NO_2)_2$
10. Na_2O_2

Page 38
Stable Ions

1. $Fe(OH)_3$
2. $CrBr_2$
3. $Cu_3(PO_4)_2$
4. $Co_2(SO_4)_3$
5. $CoSO_4$
6. MnO
7. Cu_2CO_3
8. $Cr(CH_3COO)_3$
9. CuCN
10. $NiSO_4$

Page 39
Determining Bond Type

1. polar covalent
2. ionic
3. nonpolar covalent
4. polar covalent
5. ionic
6. polar covalent
7. nonpolar covalent
8. nonpolar covalent
9. ionic
10. either polar covalent or ionic as the difference is 2.1, which is the boundary between the two types of bonds

Page 40
Lewis Structures

1. ·Ca·
2. :Ï:
3. ·Ö:
4. :Ne:
5. Ḃ·
6. :Cl—F:
7. H—Ö—Cl:
8. :F—N—F: / :F:
9. ·S̈=c=S̈·
10.
H / H—C—Ö—H / H

Page 41
Chemical Compound Crossword

Across

1. dash
5. polar
6. equal
7. ionic
9. electronegativity
12. double
13. NO
14. atom
16. ions
17. zero
19. Lewis
21. pair
22. dot

Down

2. stable
3. electron
4. anion
8. cation
9. element
10. two
11. nonpolar
15. triple
18. eight
20. share

Page 46
Review

1. B
2. B
3. A
4. D
5. C
6. B
7. C
8. $C_2H_5OH + 3O_2 \rightarrow 2CO_2 + 3H_2O$
9. The energy level of ethanol is higher than that of carbon monoxide.

ANSWER KEY cont'd.

Page 47
Balancing Equations

1. $2Na + Cl_2 \rightarrow 2NaCl$
2. $2NaN_3 \rightarrow 2Na + 3N_2$
3. $NO_2 + O_2 \rightarrow NO + O_3$
4. $2LiOH + CO_2 \rightarrow Li_2CO_3 + H_2O$
5. $N_2 + 3H_2 \rightarrow 2NH_3$
6. $CH_4 + 2O_2 \rightarrow CO_2 + 2H_2O$
7. $2ZnS + 3O_2 \rightarrow 2ZnO + 2SO_2$
8. $2C_8H_{18} + 25O_2 \rightarrow 16CO_2 + 18H_2O$
9. $SiCl_4 + 2Mg \rightarrow 2MgCl_2 + Si$
10. $CO + 2H_2 \rightarrow CH_3OH$
11. $Al_2O_3 + 3H_2SO_4 \rightarrow Al_2(SO_4)_3 + 3H_2O$
12. $3Cu + 8HNO_3 \rightarrow 3Cu(NO_3)_2 + 4H_2O + 2NO$

Page 48
Translating Word Equations

1. nickel + lead nitrate → nickel nitrate + lead
   $Ni + Pb(NO_3)_2 \rightarrow Ni(NO_3)_2 + Pb$
2. aluminum + nickel(II) iodide → aluminum iodide + nickel
   $2Al + 3NiI_2 \rightarrow 2AlI_3 + 3Ni$
3. water → hydrogen + oxygen
   $2H_2O \rightarrow 2H_2 + O_2$
4. sodium phosphate + calcium nitrate → sodium nitrate + calcium phosphate
   $2Na_3PO_4 + 3Ca(NO_3)_2 \rightarrow 6NaNO_3 + Ca_3(PO_4)_2$
5. ammonia + oxygen → nitrogen monoxide + water vapor
   $4NH_3 + 5O_2 \rightarrow 4NO + 6H_2O$
6. iron(II) hydroxide + hydrogen peroxide → iron(III) hydroxide
   $2Fe(OH)_2 + H_2O_2 \rightarrow 2Fe(OH)_3$

Page 49
Types of Chemical Reactions

1. $6Na + Fe_2O_3 \rightarrow 3Na_2O + 2Fe$; single-replacement
2. $H_2 + Br_2 \rightarrow 2HBr$; synthesis
3. $2AgCl \rightarrow 2Ag + Cl_2$; decomposition
4. $2C_2H_6 + 7O_2 \rightarrow 4CO_2 + 6H_2O$; combustion
5. $CaO + H_2O \rightarrow Ca(OH)_2$; synthesis

6. $Ca(OH)_2 + 2HCl \rightarrow CaCl_2 + 2H_2O$; double-replacement
7. $Fe(NO_3)_3 + 3LiOH \rightarrow 3LiNO_3 + Fe(OH)_3$; double-replacement
8. $4Fe + 3O_2 \rightarrow 2Fe_2O_3$; synthesis
9. $C_{12}H_{22}O_{11} + 12O_2 \rightarrow 12CO_2 + 11H_2O$; combustion

Page 50
Predicting the Products

1. hydrogen iodide → hydrogen + iodine;
   $2HI \rightarrow H_2 + I_2$
2. aluminum + oxygen → aluminum oxide;
   $4Al + 3O_2 \rightarrow 2Al_2O_3$
3. sodium bromide + chlorine → sodium chloride + bromine; $2NaBr + Cl_2 \rightarrow 2NaCl + Br_2$
4. butane + oxygen → carbon dioxide + water;
   $2C_5H_{10} + 15O_2 \rightarrow 10CO_2 + 10H_2O$
5. zinc + copper(II) sulfate → zinc sulfate + copper; $Zn + CuSO_4 \rightarrow ZnSO_4 + Cu$
6. barium chlorate → barium chloride + oxygen;
   $Ba(ClO_3)_2 \rightarrow BaCl_2 + 3O_2$
7. copper(II) sulfate + ammonium sulfide → copper(II) sulfide + ammonium sulfate;
   $CuSO_4 + (NH_4)_2S \rightarrow CuS + (NH_4)_2SO_4$
8. oxygen + methanol → carbon dioxide + water;
   $3O_2 + 2CH_3OH \rightarrow 2CO_2 + 4H_2O$
9. water → hydrogen + oxygen; $2H_2O \rightarrow 2H_2 + O_2$
10. magnesium + nitrogen → magnesium nitride;
    $3Mg + N_2 \rightarrow Mg_3N_2$

Page 51
Energy Changes I

1. potential energy of the reactant(s)
2. activation energy
3. potential energy of the activated complex
4. potential energy of the product(s)
5. This is an example of an exothermic reaction because the potential energy level of the product(s) is less than that of the reactant(s).
6. add a catalyst

ANSWER KEY cont'd.

Page 52
Energy Changes II
1. This graph represents an endothermic reaction because the potential energy level of the product, C, is higher than the combined potential energy level of the reactants, A and B.
2. The X should be placed at the peak of the curve.
3. The dashed line should be drawn to show that the "hump" is lowered.
4. The arrow should extend from the base of the graph to the portion of the curve labeled A + B.
5. The arrow should extend from a point level with the portion of the curve labeled A + B to the portion of the curve labeled C.

Page 53
Chemical Equilibrium
1. The equilibrium will shift toward the left.
2. The equilibrium will shift toward the left.
3. The equilibrium will shift toward the right.
4. The equilibrium will shift toward the right.
5. The equilibrium will shift toward the right.
6. Decrease the concentrations of the products.
7. Increasing the pressure would have no effect as the volumes of reactants and products are equal.
8. There is not enough information to answer this question.

Page 58
Review
1. D   2. B   3. C   4. B
5. A   6. C
7. A mole is defined as the number of atoms of carbon in exactly 12 grams of carbon-12.
8. A balanced chemical equation indicates the mole ratios of reactants and products. These mole ratios are required to solve stoichiometry problems.

Page 59
Moles, Molar Mass, and Avogadro's Number
1. 2.4 mol   2. 0.06 mol
3. 0.18 mol   4. 1.3 mol
5. 8.2 mol   6. 207.2 g
7. 76.8 g   8. 1259.4 g
9. 616 g   10. 369.8 g
11. 1.8×10^{23} atoms
12. 4.2×10^{23} atoms
13. 2.4×10^{24} atoms
14. 2.4×10^{24} molecules
15. 1.3×10^{-10} mol
16. 95 mol
17. 0.58 mol
18. 30.9 mol

Page 60
Percentage Composition
1. 50.05% S, 49.95% O
2. 35.00% N, 5.05% H, 59.96% O
3. 39.99% C, 6.73% H, 53.28% O
4. 39.99% C, 6.73% H, 53.28% O
5. 63.70% Pb, 14.77% C, 1.86% H, 19.67% O

Page 61
Empirical Formulas
1. FeS
2. $PbCl_2$
3. $K_2Cr_2O_7$
4. BaN_2O_6 or $Ba(NO_3)_2$
5. $N_2H_8CO_3$ or $(NH_4)_2CO_3$

Page 62
Molecular Formulas
1. NO_2 2. C_6H_6
3. P_4O_{10} 4. N_2H_4
5. $O_3C_3N_3Cl_3$

ANSWER KEY cont'd.

Page 63
Molarity
1. 0.83 M
2. 1.75 M
3. 0.816 M
4. 2.5 g
5. 11 g

Page 64
Mole-Mass Problems
1. 62.5 mol
2. 2000 g or 2 kg
3. 40 mol
4. 1.760 kg
5. 810 g

Page 65
Volume-Volume Problems
1. $2CO + O_2 \rightarrow 2CO_2$
2. 315 mL
3. 6.25 L
4. 1.25 L
5. Not all of the carbon monoxide will be converted because not enough oxygen is present to react completely with 425 mL of carbon monoxide. Oxygen is a limiting reactant because 212.5 mL is required.

Page 66
Mass-Mass Problems
1. $NH_4NO_3 \rightarrow N_2O + 2H_2O$
2. 120 g
3. 54.0 g
4. 33.0 g

Page 67
Ideal Gas Law
1. 1.22 atm
2. 6.17 L
3. 3.98 atm
4. 0.90 atm

Page 68
Graham's Law of Effusion
1. N_2 travels faster according to Graham's law of effusion because it has a smaller molar mass.
2. H_2 travels four times faster than O_2.
3. $\dfrac{465 \text{ m}}{\text{s}}$
4. $\dfrac{71.0 \text{ g}}{\text{mol}}$
5. $\dfrac{169 \text{ g}}{\text{mol}}$

Page 72
Review
1. B   2. C   3. B   4. D
5. A   6. D   7. B
8. Ammonia does not form hydroxide ions to be considered an Arrhenius base, but it does accept protons so that it is classified as a Brønsted-Lowry base.
9. 2.07 M

Page 73
Brønsted-Lowry Acids and Bases
1. H_2SO_4 –acid; H_2O –base
2. CO_3^{2-} –base, H_2O –acid
3. NH_4^+ –acid; OH^- –base
4. $HCOOH$ –acid; CH_3COO^- –base
5. H_2O –base; CH_3COOH –acid
6. HCN –acid; H_2O –base
7. $C_6H_5NH_2$ –base, H_2O –acid
8. Either H_2O can be labeled the acid; the other H_2O must then be the base.

ANSWER KEY cont'd.

Page 74
Conjugate Acids and Bases

1. HCO_3^- and CO_3^{2-}
   NH_3 and NH_4^+

2. HCl and Cl^-
   H_2O and H_3O^+

3. CH_3COOH and CH_3COO^-
   H_2O and H_3O^+

4. $HOCl$ and ClO^-
   NH_3 and NH_4^+

5. H_2SO_4 and HSO_4^-
   OH^- and H_2O

6. HPO_4^{2-}
7. CN^-
8. OH^-
9. $HOOCCOO^-$
10. HF
11. H_2O
12. H_3O^+
13. NH_4^+

Page 75
pH

Sample	pH	$[H_3O^+]$	$[OH^-]$	Acidic or Basic
rain water	5	1×10^{-5} M	1×10^{-9} M	acidic
window-cleaning liquid	11	1×10^{-11} M	1×10^{-3} M	basic
stomach contents	2	1×10^{-2} M	1×10^{-12} M	acidic
black coffee	5	1×10^{-5} M	1×10^{-9} M	acidic
hand soap	10	1×10^{-10} M	1×10^{-4} M	basic
apple juice	3	1×10^{-3} M	1×10^{-11} M	acidic
drain cleaner	13	1×10^{-13} M	1×10^{-1} M	basic
baking soda	9	1×10^{-9} M	1×10^{-5} M	basic
antacid	8	1×10^{-8} M	1×10^{-6} M	basic
pure water	7	1×10^{-7} M	1×10^{-7} M	neutral

Page 76
Molarity and Normality

1. 0.6 N
2. 2.4 N
3. 2 M
4. 32 g
5. 1.65 M, 3.3 N
6. 24.4 g

Page 77
Titration

1. 6.67×10^{-3} M
2. 0.33 M
3. 75 mL
4. 150 mL
5. 2.2×10^{-5} M

Page 78
Acid-Base Word Search

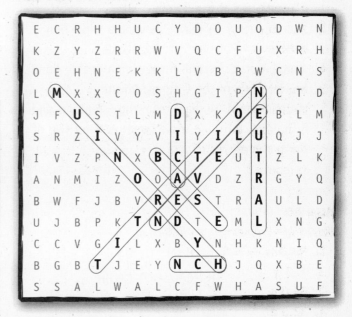

1. hydronium
2. base
3. titration
4. HCN
5. neutral
6. acid
7. eleven

ANSWER KEY cont'd.

Page 83

Review

1. B **2.** D **3.** D **4.** C
5. A **6.** B **7.** D

8. As an alkane, ethane is a saturated hydrocarbon and cannot react with Cl_2 because it does not contain double bonds that can be broken. In contrast, ethene is an unsaturated hydrocarbon whose double bonds can be broken in a reaction with Cl_2.

Page 84

Hydrocarbons

1. structure must be drawn showing only single bonds between C atoms; alkane
2. structure must be drawn showing a double bond between two of the C atoms; alkene
3. structure must be drawn showing a triple bond between two of the C atoms; alkyne
4. structure must be drawn showing a double bond between two of the C atoms; alkene
5. structure must be drawn showing 5 C atoms and 8 H atoms with one triple bond between two of the C atoms

Page 85

Functional Groups
Names of Covalent Compounds

1. carboxylic acid

2. ketone

3. alcohol

4. ether

5. ester

Page 86

Isomers

1. Any two alkane structures that contain 4 C atoms, 10 H atoms, and only single bonds are correct as long as they have different structural formulas.

2. No, they cannot be isomers because they must have the same kinds and number of atoms. In other words, they must have the same molecular formulas.

3. These properties depend on how the atoms are arranged in a molecule. Because they have different arrangements of atoms, isomers have different properties.

4. Any two alcohol structures that contain 3 C atoms, 8 H atoms, and 1 O atom with the —OH functional group attached to a carbon atom, as long as the functional group is not shown in the same position in both structural formulas.

5. Any structure that contains 5 C atoms, 8 H atoms, and 2 O atoms and that follows bonding rules but has a different arrangement of the atoms is correct.

ANSWER KEY cont'd.

Page 87

Names and Structures of Hydrocarbons

1. 3,3-dimethyl-1-pentene
2. 3,3-dimethyl-1-butyne
3.

4.

5.

Page 88

Names and Structures of Compounds with Functional Groups

1. 2-pentanone
2. 3-hexanol
3. butanoic acid
4.

5.

Page 89

Substitution and Addition Reactions

1. Alkanes are saturated molecules, having only single bonds between their carbon atoms. Therefore, there are no multiple bonds to break so that atoms or molecules can be added. However, the hydrogen atoms can be replaced by another atom or molecule so that a substitution reaction can take place.

2.

3a.

3b.

3c. substitution reaction

4.

Page 90

Condensation and Hydrolysis Reactions

1.

2.

Answer Key
Chemistry, SV 0424-7

3.

H-N-CH$_2$-CH$_2$-CH$_2$-CH$_2$-CH$_2$-CH$_2$-N-C-CH$_2$-CH$_2$-CH$_2$-CH$_2$-C-OH + H$_2$O

Page 91
Polymers

1. —O—CH$_2$—CH$_2$—O—CH$_2$—CH$_2$—O—

2.

3.

Page 95
Review

1. B   **2.** A   **3.** D   **4.** D

5. B   **6.** C

7. They both consist of two protons and two neutrons.

8. Fission involves the breaking apart of nuclei while fusion is a process in which nuclei are combined. Both release a tremendous amount of energy.

Page 96
Nuclear Equations

1. $^{4}_{2}$He

2. $^{234}_{91}$Pa

3. $^{0}_{-1}e$

4. $^{256}_{101}$Md

5. $^{139}_{56}$Ba

6. $^{1}_{0}$n

7. $^{239}_{93}$Np $\rightarrow$ $^{0}_{-1}e$ + $^{239}_{94}$Pu

8. $^{22}_{11}$Na + $^{0}_{-1}e$ $\rightarrow$ $^{22}_{10}$Ne

9. $^{238}_{92}$U $\rightarrow$ $^{4}_{2}$He + $^{234}_{90}$Th

10. 4^{1}_{1}H $\rightarrow$ $2^{0}_{+1}e$ + $^{4}_{2}$He

Page 97
Fission and Fusion

1. $^{235}_{92}$U + $^{1}_{0}$n $\rightarrow$ $^{144}_{55}$Cs + $^{90}_{37}$Rb + 2^{1}_{0}n

2. $^{235}_{92}$U + $^{1}_{0}$n $\rightarrow$ $^{87}_{35}$Br + $^{146}_{57}$La + 3^{1}_{0}n

3. $^{21}_{10}$Ne + $^{4}_{2}$He $\rightarrow$ $^{24}_{12}$Mg + $^{1}_{0}$n; This is a fusion reaction because a larger nucleus is made from two smaller nuclei that are combined.

4. 2^{3}_{2}He $\rightarrow$ 2^{1}_{1}H + $^{4}_{2}$He

5. $^{239}_{94}$Pu $\rightarrow$ $^{4}_{2}$He + $^{235}_{92}$U

6. $^{208}_{82}$Pb + $^{58}_{26}$Fe $\rightarrow$ $^{1}_{0}$n + $^{265}_{108}$Hs

Page 98
Half-Life Problems

1. 72.3 days

2. 40.1 days

3. 40,005 years old

4. 9.6 mg

5. about $3\frac{1}{2}$ half-lives

6. about 6.25 g

Page 99
Nuclear Chemistry Puzzle

1. fission   **2.** half-lives

3. decay   **4.** balanced

5. alpha particle   **6.** helium

7. positron   **8.** radioactivity

Page 104
Review

1. B   **2.** D   **3.** C   **4.** A

5. D   **6.** B   **7.** D

8. Oxidation involves the loss of electrons, while reduction involves the gain of electrons.

9. An electrochemical cell consists of two electrodes separated by an electrolyte. An electrode is a conductor that connects with a nonmetallic part of an electrical circuit. An electrolyte is a substance that dissolves in water to produce a solution that conducts electricity.

Page 105
Oxidation Numbers
1. Au: 0
2. H: +1; O: −2
3. Mg: +2
4. K: +1; O: −2
5. B: +3; F: −1
6. N: −3; H: +1
7. Ca: +2; O: −2; H: +1
8. S: +7; O: −2
9. Fe: +3; C: +4; O: −2
10. Na: +1; Bi: +5; O: −2
11. Na: +1; H: +1; C: +4; O: −2
12. Cr: +6; O: −2
13. N: −3; H: +1; N: +5; O: −2
14. H: +1; P: +5; O: −2

Page 106
Redox Equations
1. This is a redox reaction because the oxidation number of O changes from −2 to 0, indicating that it has been oxidized. The oxidation number of N changes from +5 to +3, indicating that it has been reduced.
2. This is not a redox reaction because the oxidation numbers of all the atoms remain unchanged.
3. This is a redox reaction because the oxidation number of S changes from −2 to +6, indicating that it has been oxidized. The oxidation number of N changes from +5 to +4, indicating that it has been reduced.
4. This is a redox reaction because the oxidation number of Zn changes from 0 to +2, indicating that it has been oxidized. The oxidation number

of Cu changes from +2 to 0, indicating that it has been reduced.
5. This is not a redox reaction because the oxidation numbers of all the atoms remain unchanged.
6. This is a redox reaction because the oxidation number of Mn changes from +7 to +2, indicating that it has been reduced. The oxidation number of Fe changes from +2 to +3, indicating that it has been oxidized.
7. This is a redox reaction because the oxidation number of Fe changes from 0 to +3, indicating that it has been oxidized. The oxidation number of O changes from 0 to −2, indicating that it has been reduced.

Page 107
Activity Series
1. This reaction will occur: $Mg + Pb(NO_3)_2 \rightarrow Pb + Mg(NO_3)_2$. Mg is oxidized as its oxidation number changes from 0 to +2, while Pb is reduced as its oxidation number changes from +2 to 0.
2. This reaction will occur: $2Na + 2H_2O \rightarrow 2NaOH + H_2$. Na is oxidized as its oxidation number changes from 0 to +1, while H is reduced as its oxidation number changes from +1 to 0.
3. No redox reaction will occur.
4. This reaction will occur: $2Al + 3Zn(NO_3)_2 \rightarrow 3Zn + 2Al(NO_3)_3$. Al is oxidized as its oxidation number changes from 0 to +3, while Zn is reduced as its oxidation number changes from +2 to 0.
5. No redox reaction will occur.
6. This reaction will occur: $Mg + 2HCl \rightarrow H_2 + MgCl_2$. Mg is oxidized as its oxidation number changes from 0 to +2, while H is reduced as its oxidation number changes from +1 to 0.
7. This reaction will occur: $Ni + CuSO_4 \rightarrow Cu + NiSO_4$. Ni is oxidized as its oxidation number changes from 0 to +2, while Cu is reduced as its oxidation number changes from +2 to 0.

Pages 108–109

Electrochemical Cells

1. MnO_2: :Mn: +4; O: −2; H_2O: H: +1; O: −2;
   Mn_2O_3: Mn: +3; O: −2; OH^-: O: −2; H: +1

2. Mn

3. This reaction occurs at the cathode because Mn is reduced as evidenced by the change in its oxidation number: +4 to +3.

4. The MnO_2 will gradually be converted to Mn_2O_3 as the reduction reaction continues.

5. Zn: 0; OH^-: O: −2; H: +1; $Zn(OH)_2$: Zn: 2+; O: −2; H: +1

6. Zn

7. This reaction occurs at the anode because Zn is oxidized as evidenced by the change in its oxidation number: 0 to +2.

8. The Zn will gradually be converted to $Zn(OH)_2$ as the oxidation reaction continues.

Page 110

Electrolytic Cells

1. $Ag \rightarrow Ag^+ + e^-$

2. $Ag^+ + e^- \rightarrow Ag$

3. The battery supplies the electrical energy needed to bring about the nonspontaneous redox reactions.

4. The silver strip will slowly dissolve as Ag atoms are oxidized to Ag^+ ions.

5. The prefix *electro-* indicates that electricity is used as the source of energy to drive the process. The suffix *-plating* indicates that an object is plated or coated with a layer of metal.